S0-AUD-030

DISCARDED
Library
Western Wyoming Community College

Out Here on Soap Creek

977.703
F1120
1982

Out Here on Soap Creek

AN AUTOBIOGRAPHY *by* Inez McAlister Faber

The Iowa State University Press / Ames

© 1982 The Iowa State University Press. All rights reserved. Composed by Compositors, Cedar Rapids, Iowa. Printed by The Iowa State University Press, Ames, Iowa 50010. No part of this book may be reproduced in any form, by photostat, microfilm, xerography, or any other means, or incorporated into any information retrieval system, electronic or mechanical, without the written permission of the copyright owner.

First edition, 1982

Library of Congress Cataloging in Publication Data
Faber, Inez McAlister, 1897–
  Out Here on Soap Creek.

    1. Faber, Inez McAlister, 1897–   . 2. Iowa—Biography. 3. Farm life—Iowa. I. Title.
CT275.F14A36   977.7′03′0924 [B]   81–23682
ISBN 0–8138–1286–0   AACR2

5

6

To my family

7

9

8

From the Family Album ...

Frontispiece: Our home in Urbana Township, Monroe County, Iowa. December 1955.

1: Inez McAlister, early 1900s.

2: Inez and Dick Faber, 1922.

3: Vaughn and Charles, 1930.

4: Irvin and Bruce, 1941.

5: Dick, his sister Lucy and brother Ruben, their parents, Inez, and Farrie (Ruben's wife). *In front,* the Faber cousins, Dallas and Dean; Vaughn; and Charles. 1927.

6: *Front row:* Irvin, Barbara Harvey (cousin), Skippy, Wayne Harvey (cousin), and Bruce. *Back row:* Vaughn, Inez, Charles, and Dick. Summer 1942.

7: Dick and Inez, ready for Sunday School, mid-1940s.

8: Bruce, Inez, Irvin, Charles, and Vaughn, 1978.

9: Inez McAlister Faber.

Contents

Introduction

Perhaps this is not an autobiography in the true sense of the word, since it is a collection of columns selected from my newspaper writings. Yet it might be called autobiographical because the columns recall many stories of my earlier life as well as comment on the period in which they were written.

In 1927 we lived on an Appanoose County farm ten miles east of Centerville, Iowa. At that time I acquired an ancient typewriter and began writing news for the *Des Moines Register and Tribune* and the *Centerville Iowegian*. Soon Mr. J. S. Russell, farm editor of the *Register and Tribune*, asked me to write farm feature articles for the Sunday *Register*. I consulted Mr. J. M. Beck, publisher of the *Iowegian*, who agreed to use a farm feature article each Tuesday. I found material for many interesting stories, most of it from Appanoose, Davis, Monroe, and Wapello counties although I also used material from as far as Wayne, Mahaska, and Marion counties and sometimes farther afield.

Later I wrote Mr. Russell suggesting I write a column for farm women to be published on the *Tribune's* new farm page. In his reply he hinted that he wasn't too much interested in columns, but he flattered me by writing that he thought I could make one interesting if anybody could. I took that to mean "yes" and promptly sent him two columns, signed Elizabeth Beresford. Elizabeth was for my mother and Beresford was the maiden name of one of my mother's great-grandmothers who was born in the Kentucky wilderness; was widowed by the war of 1812 and left with five small daughters; moved to the new settlement in Washington County, Indiana; and came in 1846 with some of her children to Urbana Township, Monroe County, in the new state of Iowa, where she lived until her death in 1862.

The columns told of our life on the farm; our sons; their pets;

the livestock; my parents and their pioneer ancestors; childhood memories and playmates; the sandpile; the swing; the maples that I loved; the thrill of living in the home where my father was born. Often I wrote of our small hometown of Blakesburg in Adams Township, Wapello County, Iowa, just over the county line from my parent's home in Urbana Township, Monroe County.

Mr. Russell called the newly born column "A Farm Woman Speaks Up." Readers wrote of interestings happenings in their childhood and of their homes and children.

Again I talked with Mr. Beck. He agreed to use a column each week in the *Iowegian*. I called it "Out Here on the Farm," signing the initials E. D. W. When we left Appanoose County in 1934 and moved back to Monroe County the title was changed to *Out Here on Soap Creek* and signed Inez Faber—by that time everybody knew who was writing it. Mr. J. Frank Smith drew a picture for the heading of my new column. Having never seen me he pictured me with a beautiful pug nose instead of the enormous beak I possess.

The *Iowegian* purchased a new dictionary and Mr. Beck gave me the old one, which has been one of my most useful and treasured possessions (although it has become somewhat shabby) during the forty-five years it has remained on my desk.

Back in Urbana Township once more, I began writing "Unimportant Cogitations" for Mr. Howard Smith of the *Moravia Tribune* and found him just as willing to help as my other editors. Fred Raymond of the *Blakesburg Excelsior,* a longtime acquaintance of the family, used my column "Off the Reel!" and also asked me to write articles about Blakesburg's Corn Carnival for the *Excelsior.* For a time I also wrote "Musings of a Soap Creeker" for the *Albia Republican.*

My column writing days came to an end one foggy day in Missouri in February 1951. My husband, Dick; our son, Irvin; and I were on our way to a hog sale. Because of the fog Irvin couldn't drive very fast. He hadn't wanted to miss school on the day of a rather important test, but we thought we had to have a driver.

Not far south of the Iowa-Missouri line a big truck came out of a side road just ahead of us. We hit the truck, our front bumper catching on the license plate and dragging us along. As the truck gained speed the plate broke loose and we whirled around and went off over an embankment. Irvin clung tightly to the steering wheel with both hands, bouncing up and down as our pickup struck the ground with great force and landed on its right side. There was a jolt and a feeling of almost unbearable pain as my head struck the upper part of the door frame and Dick's knee jabbed into my side.

As Irvin was on the upper side, he managed to crawl out the open window of the door nearest him. Some passersby helped pull me up and out the same window. I am not sure how Dick got outside. I was cold and sleepy and my knees were skinned, but I managed to crawl up the embankment to the roadside.

Soon the sheriff came and took me to the hospital. Irvin and Dick stayed with the pickup until it was towed to a garage where its injuries were treated.

Irvin had some neck and shoulder injuries. Dick had a dislocated shoulder and a bad bump on the back of his head. My ribs were dislocated, torn loose and apart. The blow to my head above the right eye caused a brain concussion and broke off the molars on the opposite side of my head. Many of the vertebrae were dislocated, and my head was twisted to one side. I was hardly worth saving, but you know how doctors are. They think that while there is life there is hope.

Before I could be up and about my son Vaughn's wife, Patty, came to do some sweeping and the necessary cleaning. Three-year-old Cathy shut the heavy stair door on her fingers and fainted. To lie there and not be able to go pick her up was the most helpless feeling I ever had.

Finally, enough of me was put back together that I could sit in a chair and get around some. The arthritis, which had been in my knees for years, had affected my voice box where it combined with my asthma to give me a permanent hoarseness. The best thing about the accident was that I never had to make any more speeches. The bad thing was that it put an end to my pounding on the old Remington, sewing on the sewing machine, driving the car, washing windows, and many other things.

Old age made its inroads as the thirty years passed. We no longer kept livestock or poultry; the house was heated by electricity, so sawing wood and carrying out ashes was required only for the fireplace; and although we no longer had to go half a mile for the mail but just to the corner of the yard, winter became a difficult time for us. We began going home with one of the sons after our Christmas dinner and gift exchange to spend the month of January.

Dick lived until January 7, 1974, exactly forty years after the death of my father. Since then I have been here alone on Pine Tree Hill. Tall elm trees have taken over what was once my flower garden. Many of the roses, iris, and tulips are dead. The grass remains unmowed. Although I continue the battle with hoe, hatchet, and corn knife I never manage to conquer all the weeds and elm sprouts.

The minibus comes out from Albia for senior citizens on Fridays. For many years if I couldn't get all the trips to the bank, grocery, doctor, etc., done on Fridays I would stay a few days at the hotel—such as the time I was having dental work and needed to be there every day. After Christmas each year I shut off the heat with the exception of the kitchen and the two bathrooms and went to Kentucky with Charles or to Cedar Rapids with Bruce or Irvin. If I went to Kentucky, in three or four weeks I would be homesick and fly back to be met at Cedar Rapids and stay with Bruce or Irvin. In more recent years I have kept an apartment at Albia where I stay in winter and overnight any time I need to be in town. I visit my sons' homes in summertime.

Vaughn remains a farmer, using huge machinery that bears small resemblance to the implements Barney and Old Roger used to pull. Charles is a member of the faculty of the University of Kentucky. Bruce taught high school history after two years in the Air Force. Later he worked for the Internal Revenue Service for several years but became disabled and had to retire.

Irvin is an electrical engineer in Cedar Rapids. He has not lost his love for rural life; he has a tree farm nearby where he, his wife, his daughters, and friends spend vacations and many weekends. Their free time is spent caring for Christmas trees. Someday they plan to retire and live on the farm permanently. I wonder, will they rest any more then than they do during vacations? Each year I sell Christmas trees to people who come here for them. Others are sold at Irvin's home and to dealers in Cedar Rapids and in this area.

It has been a good life. The four sons have given me twenty-one grandchildren, three of them boys. The sixteen great-grandchildren are evenly divided. Christmas is the high point of the year, although it has been some time since all the family have been here at once.

Whether I am at the Albia apartment, visiting one of the sons, or with friends of other days, home is here on the farm with my memories.

Out Here on Soap Creek

1

The Early Years

Home was eight rooms on the south side of the road under the maple trees. A picket fence enclosed the yard. Two rows of maples lined the road on either side from the schoolhouse at the crossroads west—past the big hog pasture that once was one of Grandpa McAlister's orchards; past Grandma's garden, now a tangle of berry vines, rose bushes, pear, peach, and cherry trees with hop vines climbing everywhere; past the house, the woodlot, the barn and barn lot; and along the horse pasture all the way to the Red Bridge.

Locust trees had shaded the house and yard until the maples grew large enough to take over for them. That was before I was born, but the locust stumps were there still when I was in the midteens. In the backyard were four huge elms. Papa's sister, Aunt Annie Van Cleave, said that at the time of her marriage in 1879 the elms were no larger around than her wrist.

In the 1850s, 1860s, and 1870s my grandparents ran a tavern. Unless your ancestors came from Virginia you might think they sold liquor, but they didn't. They kept travelers overnight or often over the weekend, for in those days many people did not travel on the Sabbath. Once a number of people came late on a Saturday evening. Grandmother discovered she didn't have enough butter for their Sunday dinner and supper. Grandpa would not permit her to churn on the Sabbath. Nobody ever argued with Grandpa, so she managed somehow without butter.

Often their guests were drovers taking cattle, hogs, or sheep to market at Keosauqua. People on their way west to settle sometimes were overtaken by winter and stayed there until spring. Others ran out of money and stayed a few weeks or months working for Grandpa, Mr. Phinney, or Fielding Barnes.

The four bedrooms upstairs and the entire west wing of the

house were kept for travelers. After the railroad came the west wing was no longer needed. Part of it was moved to the west edge of the yard and became a coal house and a shelter for the old McCormick reaper, once a prized possession but now replaced by a more modern binder. The other two rooms of the west wing were moved farther back to the south edge of the woodlot. One room housed the top buggy and the sleigh with its pretty red lining. The other became a cow shed with the opening where the fireplace had been serving as an entrance.

There had been several small guest houses, one of them on the eighty acres across the road that now belonged to Uncle Frank. It was a log cabin with a shed kitchen. His tenants who farmed the eighty lived in it. Another log cabin near our barn was used as a corncrib. A well and some rocks that had been the foundation of a house remained over in the horse pasture, across the ditch southeast of our barn.

Another cottage had stood near the road along the east edge of the cow pasture just west of Phinney's red brick house. In this small house Grandpa's brother Rob's wife and baby had died of smallpox while brother Rob was a soldier in the Union army. Grandpa had tried to enlist but could not pass the physical. His brothers, his sisters' husbands, and several nephews were with the Indiana volunteers. Some of them were prisoners. When the half-starved prisoners were released at the end of the war, one nephew was so weak that he had to stand by the prison gate and watch the others leave for the long walk home. He never got back to Indiana. It was thought that he might have been one of those drowned in the explosion and sinking of a steamship that was bringing sick and wounded home. He was seventeen years old.

Grandpa's father had been in the Mexican War, and his mother's father had fought in the Revolutionary War and some of the French and Indian Wars. Tales of adventures and hardships in these wars were part of the family lore. My grandmother died the year before I was born; my grandfather had died four years earlier.

When I was young there were still peddlers, dark-complexioned men with huge packs on their backs, walking through the countryside. They would walk from Ottumwa; spend the night at our house; and go on from there to Foster, Moravia, and Albia. Years afterward one of our sons met a merchant in Cedar Rapids who had traveled this route many times when he first came to America from the old country—Syria, I believe it was. No doubt he had stayed overnight at our house many times.

Perhaps my earliest memory was sleeping upstairs while the fireplace was torn out, a new front door installed, and other repair work done. I remember only the sleeping upstairs and some plastering that was being done. I must have been almost two years old, for it was before the birth of my brother who was two years and two months younger than I. Since I kept trying to get somebody to tell me how to read the *Blakesburg Excelsior* and the *Youth's Companion,* my mother bought me a set of ABC blocks. I was told I would have to know the letters to be able to read. That didn't take long. I don't remember that anyone complained as I kept asking, "What is this letter?" and "What is this one?" until I had learned them all. Big brother Bert, now nine years old, began teaching me how to spell. The first word I learned was Mississippi; then I learned Missouri and a great many other and shorter words that I found more useful during the next few years of my life.

By the time I was three I was begging to be allowed to go to school. Several times my mother would say, "You can go now," and I would go out the front gate and start down the path under the maples toward the little white schoolhouse where the big kids were learning such fascinating things. With my slate and pencil in one hand and Bert's old third reader clutched in the other and wearing a clean dress and my sunbonnet on my head, I was very happy. But I never seemed to get started in time. Always I met Bert and some of his friends on the way home before I was halfway to the schoolhouse. One afternoon Mamma said I could go back to school with Bert after he had eaten his lunch. I felt very important sitting with my cousin Gertie, who was one of the big girls. I was very happy.

Birdie Miller was the teacher that spring. She boarded at Mrs. Stocker's and passed our house on the way home each evening. I would go out on the porch or maybe to the front gate and spell for her whatever new word I had learned that day. Once she asked me to say the alphabet backwards. That seemed very difficult but I did it, swinging round and round the porch post. I fear my family became very tired of hearing the alphabet backwards the next few days. However, I don't recollect their getting cross about it as they did a few years later when I had a sudden ambition to count to a million. That time they rebelled. To stop their unkind remarks I stopped counting out loud except when I was going to the mailbox, hunting eggs, going after the cows, or doing some other task where I could be alone. I can't remember whether I ever did get to a million. Probably I did. One of my lifelong failings has been to plug away stubbornly at some task that never should have been started in the first place.

When I was four years old I took my first
train ride. We went to northwest Nebraska to see Mamma's sister
Annie, who had lived out there since January 1886. Mrs. Britt
Darby and her young son Ray went with us. Mrs. Darby was a sister to Uncle Sam, Aunt Annie's husband. It was a very tiresome
trip of two days and two nights, including the wait in the Omaha
depot for the NorthWestern train we took from there.

I remember the tiresome wait in Omaha and the crowded car
we took from there. Until a number of people left the train at Valentine I had to sit in the same chair with my mother, who held Verlin in her lap. My hip was crowded against the arm of the chair,
becoming more painful by the moment. I was sitting there drowsily
in my misery when I heard the clanking of chains. As soon as they
had passed my mother called my attention to them. It was officers
with two Indians in custody. I looked up in time to see them going
out of the door and into the next car. The prisoners were hand-
cuffed and wearing leg irons that clanked as they shuffled along.

When at last we reached Rushville Aunt Annie and Uncle Sam
were waiting for us. We stayed all night in the hotel and drove out
to their place early the next morning. On the way the stage to Pine
Ridge Indian Reservation in South Dakota passed us. It didn't look
like the stagecoach I had seen pictured in one of the *Youth's Companion* stories. It was more like our spring wagons only it had four
seats instead of two.

At a fork in the road we met a small wagon, probably a buggy
without a top. A drunken little Frenchman was talking very loudly
to Uncle Sam. His speech was so broken and he talked so rapidly
that I could not understand what he was saying. I wondered why
his Indian wife didn't talk but sat there and giggled. Later Mamma
explained that she was laughing because her husband was drunk
and talking so silly. I watched the birds flying about in the willows
and hoped we would soon get to Aunt Annie's. When we did go on,
I saw my first magpie. It was sitting on a cow's back picking at a
sore. All along the twenty-three mile trip we kept meeting Indians
in covered wagons with their dogs under the wagon and perhaps
some cows or horses following. Always they got off the road when
they saw us coming—maybe to the left, maybe to the right, whichever was quicker.

When we arrived Grandpa Robinson was waiting with the cousins. I don't remember much about any of the cousins except Myrtle,
who was two years older than I. Margaret and Emmett were younger; Carl, Roy, Naomi, and Zelma were older. All but Carl had been
born in Nebraska.

I remember a little about going up to Grandpa's claim and seeing his little cave, a tiny room about four feet square and nearly as high dug out of the side of the hill beside his tiny one-room cabin. He had only to open a small door and reach in to the cool space to get food he was keeping there. If you were to come to my house today, go back into the laundry room, open the door, and walk into my cave you might guess that I first dreamed of it back there on that Nebraska hilltop some seventy-eight years ago, before I had ever heard of a refrigerator or dreamed I'd live in a house that was wired for electricity.

The only other thing I remember about that trip was the day we went to Pine Ridge to see beef issued to the Indians. Men in a wagon dumped out the beef into the middle of the dusty street, where it was cut up and divided among the waiting men. The old men began eating theirs at once. I hope they left some for their wives. The younger ones took theirs home to have it cooked.

"Go get some shooy [shoes]," Verlin, who was only two, kept yelling at the moccasin-clad redskins. Soon the Indian agent, a white man wearing a black suit, white shirt, black shoes and socks, and a funny hat, walked past. "There's some shooy. He's got some shooy," happily shouted Verlin.

We watched a young woman with a baby wrapped in a shawl on her back, as were all the dusky infants. This one was entertaining the youngster by bumping his head quite roughly against the brick wall of the building near where we were standing.

Presently Uncle Sam came and we went with him on a tour of the dusty tent village. We stopped at Red Cloud's tent, where the great warrior was sitting enthroned on an ordinary kitchen chair much like those in the Urbana Center Church back home. Some members of his family were standing modestly behind him within the tent, peering out of the open tent flap. An old warrior strode past, wearing only moccasins, a breechclout, and a blanket.

On the way back to Aunt Annie's I was very tired and thirsty. Uncle Sam stopped the team as we were fording a rock-bottomed stream, dipped into the clear water on the upstream side beside the wagon, and gave each of us a good cold drink from a tin cup he carried for just such emergencies.

Soon after the Nebraska trip we got our

first telephone. I know we had one before Aunt Lottie died in the spring of 1902. Grandpa had given his claim to cousin Carl and come back to help Uncle Silas when Aunt Lottie became so sick.

The telephone line did not extend to their house yet. I was looking out the west kitchen window. Papa was cutting some wood at the woodpile in the woodlot when I saw a man riding a sweating horse stop, say something to Papa, and turn and ride back west under the maple trees. He had ridden six miles to tell the sad news. It was the first funeral I remember attending. I recall something about yellow roses and Uncle Silas holding eleven-month-old Ronald and looking into the casket. I wondered why he was crying. I remember a little about driving back to the cemetery and somebody holding the gate open so the wagons could drive through.

Silas took our old pine cradle for Ronald. I missed the cradle very much. I liked to sit in it and daydream. At that time I didn't know the history of the cradle; I only knew I missed it greatly. My great-grandfather Smith had bought it at a farm sale; his three youngest children had been rocked in it. Then my mother and her brothers and sisters and later Bert, Verlin, and I had used it. (In 1924 I heard it had been discarded on a brush pile in Blakesburg. I went to the rescue. The trash had been set on fire, but it was wet from a recent rain and had not yet burned. My four sons and nearly all my grandchildren were rocked in that cradle.) I do not know its early history but evidently it had come from Virginia, for the pine from which it was made was not native to either Indiana or Iowa. Most of the settlers around here, like my own ancestors, had come from Virginia to Kentucky, to Indiana, and then to Iowa.

We had our telephone before the rural mail route came. Before we had rural free delivery anyone who went to town brought the mail out to the neighbors. I remember once seeing Richard Forster tie his horses to the hitching post by our front gate and come on his crutches up the path to the front door. He had brought our mail; in it was a valentine for every member of the family. Uncle Silas and Ronald were visiting Ronald's grandparents in Ottumwa and had sent each of us a valentine.

When the mail was first delivered Bert, Verlin, and I waited at our new mailbox across the road from the schoolhouse. Tip Wilson was our first mail carrier. He drove a pair of burros hitched to a cart in summer. In winter he rode in a clumsy enclosed mail wagon.

At the age of five I became a schoolgirl. All I remember about the first two-month term was that on the first day the teacher went up to her desk and picked up a box of chalk; the bottom fell out of it and chalk went all over the floor.

The next fall we had a different teacher. She boarded at our house. As her mother was dead, she had helped raise her brothers and sisters. She said they had difficulty getting one of her brothers to wash his bare feet at night before going to bed until her older sister washed them once with the scrub brush.

One time Verlin and I had colds. The weather was bad, and we were supposed to stay in the house. While Mamma was out doing the milking we had a great time playing out in the yard until we saw her coming back to the house. We ran inside, I at the back door and Verlin at the front. He was sitting on the teacher's lap by the time I burst into the room. "We wouldn't have been whipped if you had come in at the front door as I did so Mamma couldn't have seen you," he scolded me afterwards. I felt properly rebuked, not realizing Mamma had been hearing our happy voices long before she came back to the kitchen.

That winter was cold. One night a big snow came, leaving a zig-zag of drifts in front of the rail fences on either side of the road. When I started to school Mamma said to walk in the path she had told Bert to make for me. It was a very interesting path that Bert and his friend Johnny had made. Up one big drift, a huge white mountain on the south side of the road; then across the road again; and so on with a drift to climb at every angle of the rail fences. It was one of the happiest times of my life. Never before had I had such a thrilling adventure.

The big boys made a fox-and-geese ring in the snow and we five- and six-year-olds played that game with them for a while, although the fox always caught us. Somebody started to make a snowman. Somebody else had a better idea: "Let's build a fort!" That was quite a task, for the snow fort they erected was enormous and almost four feet high. Soon Bert and Luke were Washington and Cornwallis, with every boy in school being either a patriot or a redcoat. The next day Cornwallis (Luke) and his redcoats were soundly defeated. They had to surrender the fort. Bert and Johnny had soaked their ammunition (snowballs) in our rain barrel and then let them freeze overnight. I don't think Mamma knew that. She also didn't know that each of our kittens was formally baptized—by immersion—in that rain barrel every spring. Then, as now, children knew that what mothers don't know won't hurt them.

Our sister Gertie was born one hot July morning that summer. Upon awakening I didn't know where I was for a moment. Verlin and I were in the front room lying on a pallet made of folded comforters. Verlin was still asleep. Voices were coming from the kitchen. I looked in; at the breakfast table were not only Papa and Bert, Uncle Frank, Glen and Charley, and Dr. Udell with his white beard, but also some people I didn't know. Afterward I learned that they were Albert Tubaugh and Sam Byrum who had come to help with the haying, which was to start that day. Aunt Lyde and Mattie Angel were waiting on the table.

Earlier that year I had been given the task of caring for the chickens—turning the broody hens off their nests each evening to be fed and keeping the mother hens in coops with their broods. Each coop had to be tightly closed each night to keep the varmints out and opened each morning. I liked that and the task of hunting the eggs. First I went over to the hog house and looked in the straw piled in the alley way and then in the pens if there were no piggies and their mothers in them. Then I gathered all the eggs in the nests in the hen house; climbed up on the cow shed, walked along its straw roof to the old buggy shed, crept into the attic of the shed and searched the nests that were there; and climbed back across the cow shed roof. I had to look in the coal house, too.

Last of all, I went to the barn and looked in the big south hay-mow over the granaries, in all the mangers, and in the hay along the wide driveway. Then I climbed up on the manger at the west end of the barn and swung myself up by hanging on to the wide braces that supported the big hewn beam under that haymow. Once I found Mrs. Stocker's cat with a litter of kittens in a warm nest there. Blackie, our cat, found them, too. She thought they were so nice that she took two of them and raised them with her own brood of three. They were a little larger than her own Spot, Ring, and little gray Timmie. Verlin and I named the new kittens Grace and Helen, but Bert didn't like the names and changed them to Tom and Blue. Old Blue lived to be nineteen years old. It was fun climbing up to the mow, finding eggs, and playing with kittens, but next came the scary part—I had to swing myself back down again. Sometimes I would be there for quite some time before I worked up enough courage to begin the descent.

One new task I didn't like. I had to dry the dishes.

Mary King came to work for us for two weeks while Mamma was in bed. Mary was thirteen years old. Sometimes she went barefoot; once she stubbed her bare toe on a chair. "I like to do that. It feels so good when it stops hurting," she announced as she rubbed the bruised spot and bravely kept back the tears. Once long afterward Mary embarrassed me by telling at our Wednesday club that I read the stories in the *Youth's Companion*s and other magazines when I was only six. I hadn't read the continued stories, just those that were complete in each issue.

One task that was fun was shelling the seed corn before planting time each spring. Papa selected the most nearly perfect ears as he sat in the doorway of the corncrib where the light was the best. The rest of us sat grouped about him on the floor. With his knife he would take four or five kernels, selecting one or two from near the middle of the ear and the others from near the top or bottom. He would cut a notch out of each grain thus selected so he could examine the germ to see if it would grow. If it was blackened or did not look healthy, that ear was discarded. Only a few were deemed unfit for planting.

From each good ear either Papa or Mamma shelled the crooked kernels from the top and the small kernels at the lower end of the ear. These were kept to be fed to the calves or other livestock. Then Mamma would shell two rows of kernels from each ear for us to make our task easier, and we shelled the seed into the big bushel measure or the half bushel pail. Whenever either of these was full, one of us would hold the big grain sack for Papa as he emptied the corn into it. We used the clean red cobs to build rail fences at the sandpile or rail corncribs like Papa's down by the east hog pasture between our house and the schoolhouse. After we were through playing with them the cobs could be used for fuel. The cobs out of the horses' troughs were not very nice; their soft red fuzz was all gone. The cows ate their corn, cob and all, but we found nice ones where the pigs had been fed. Some people think pigs are dirty just because they like to lie in mud, but they are as clean as a dog or cat. Cows and poultry are very poor housekeepers, but hogs are particular about their homes.

Mamma used pine shavings to start the fire in the range. On top of them she put corncobs and then the wood. She put the lids on the stove, opened the little door in front, and lighted the kindling through the grate. We enjoyed helping pick up cobs from the hog lot. We didn't like it so well when it was rainy and we had to get cobs from the barn, for the horses had slobbered on them. Usually we had many bags—gunnysacks, we called them—of cobs stored in the coal house to be used in winter or in rainy weather.

When I was six, three former neighbor families came to visit us one day. We hadn't seen them since they had moved to the northern part of the state, so it was quite an occasion. My big brother and the boys about his age went for a trip across the fields and through the woods, leaving us smaller children to entertain the younger visitors.

The yard was full of small boys and girls, but I was most interested in Cindy. When she had lived here we had been almost inseparable. If we were not together during all our waking hours, it was neither my fault nor hers. We two soon tired of the sandpile and decided to go upstairs to play with the doll families. We slipped away quietly. We didn't want any noisy boys or bothersome smaller sisters to follow us.

As we came around the corner of the house we saw a gleam of pink at the old well. Cindy's small cousin had found a broken board and pushed it aside so he could crawl inside the curbing. He was seated calmly on the rotted platform, playing with the long unused rope and wooden bucket. I was terrified. We children were afraid of the well. Sometimes if one of the big folks was with us for protection we ventured to turn the windlass crank a few times just to see what Grandma had done when she wanted a bucket of water, but when we were alone we stayed away from that corner of the yard. I knew it was mere chance that the small creeper's weight had not broken through the weak old boards. I whispered to Cindy to tell him to come away quickly before he fell through. But my playmate was wise for her five years. Taking care of a smaller sister and two younger brothers had taught her much about the vagaries of human nature.

"He won't come if I say anything. He's terribly spoiled," she told me. Her voice was nearly as shaky as mine, yet there was a note of contempt in it. In big families like Cindy's there were no spoiled babies. "Let's pretend we have found something to play with and he will come to take it away from us," she continued. The ruse worked. The pink dress left the dangerous spot as its owner hurried to see and claim the toys we had picked up.

I don't know much about Cindy any more. I haven't seen her for years. But I have no doubt that she has managed very well. I imagine she has succeeded in whatever she tried to do, without undue conflict. Baby-tending may have been tiresome for her. Goodness knows she had her share of it! There were three children younger than the three she had under her protection the day she was at our house. But babies are much like grown-ups, even though they have not yet learned treachery, cruelty, dishonesty, and other traits common to their elders. Yes, I'll bet Cindy can fool the grown-ups just as she did the kids.

The most frightening task I had to do as a
small child was to go to the barn at night and turn out the horses
after they had eaten their hay and grain. I didn't try to go down
through the woodlot, climb over the fence by the big concrete tank,
and cross the ditch to the barn. Whatever was lurking out there in
the dark might see me. Instead I went out the front gate; down the
dark road under the maples; and across the bridge under which
lived the bad man who caught naughty little girls and boys, creep-
ing very softly and being careful that no horse stepped on my bare
feet. I climbed up on the manger and unfastened the buckles of the
halters. That was the scary time for whatever was there in the dark
could surely hear that. When the last tired horse was outside and
rolling in the barnyard dust with satisfied groans, I was over the
gate and dashing up the road toward the light from our windows as
fast as I could run. I knew tramps slept in the barn. Papa had once
accidentally stuck a pitchfork into one who had crawled under the
hay to keep warm. But I wasn't afraid of tramps. Didn't we have
them begging at the back door every day? It was the dark. As for
the bad man under the culvert, he never showed himself in daytime
except once when Verlin and I were having an argument and he was
heard at the west kitchen door. I peeked out through the keyhole
and saw his arm. He was wearing a shirt just like Bert's new one.

Whenever Gracie and Bertie came over and I walked back with
them as far as the Red Bridge with the swallows' nests underneath,
I wasn't afraid of the bad man at all. But at night it was a different
story. I tried very hard to be good, but I managed to do something
wrong nearly every day. No doubt the bad man was lying under the
culvert with the brush growing up around it and thinking how
naughty I had been.

When Bert was about twelve or thirteen he wanted a room
of his own where we couldn't get into his possessions. He took the
old walnut bed out of one of the small upstairs bedrooms and built
a desk along one wall, using cracker boxes for lumber to make
bookshelves and pigeonholes. He had a telegraph key to practice
sending, with a homemade battery that froze and broke the following winter. This room was kept locked. I found the key where he
had hidden it over the door. Often when Bert was busy in the field
I slipped inside and read his books. It wasn't the thing to do, but I
so loved to read. I made the acquaintance of *The Erie Train Boy,
Robinson Crusoe, The Wide, Wide World,* and many other fascinating books.

Somewhat later I, too, had a room of my own. It didn't have a lock and key but it had draw curtains of cretonne like that on my desk. My desk was made from a big cracker box filled with *Youth's Companion*s that my grandfather and later my mother had saved for many years. On top of the cracker box were two drawers of cherry wood saved from the big clothes press that had been torn out of the front room. Inside those drawers with the top one turned upside down over the other, I kept among other treasures the *Burlington Hawkeye* with accounts of Lincoln's death and newspapers containing the news of the assassinations of Garfield and McKinley. Grandpa Mac had given the first two to Mamma; she had saved the later ones and given them all to me. I had a little table in one corner of the room, the top somewhat worm eaten, but the top did not show with the cover on it. I had the little walnut bed that had been Grandma Mac's lounge in the front room and had been in the McAlister family before she was married—in fact before they had gone to Indiana. Did they call them Jenny Lind or spool beds? I never can remember. The cupboard held my postcard album, letters, stamp collection, railroad pencils that Ernest (my mother's half-brother) sent me from all the different railroads in the United States, cards the teachers gave for "headmarks in spelling," last day of school cards, valentines, and momentoes brought from the World's Fair in St. Louis by my uncles. Those uncles were responsible for many of the other treasures in that little cupboard—shells from Florida and other seashores, Indian beadwork, some rattlesnake rattles, some odd coins, and doll furniture and dishes. It also held the china hen on a dish from Aunt Annie (not the Nebraska aunt but Papa's sister who lived nearby and was the mother of my big cousins Gertie and Bert, who had named our Gertie and Bert after themselves). On rainy days when I didn't have anything to do after chores and the dishes and the sweeping and dusting were done, I loved to lie up there listening to the rain on the tin porch roof and read *Youth's Companion*s that had been printed many years before I was born. As I grew older I read the continued stories, too, but many of the chapters were missing.

It was interesting for me as a child to listen to my parents and their friends and relatives talk about bygone days. Why couldn't I have been born one hundred or even fifty years earlier, when so many wonderful things happened? There was talk of wild turkeys; of the long walk to Hummaconna after a post office was established there; of the trip from Indiana with the ox team; of

Great-grandmother hanging the milk in a pail under the axle in the morning and finding her butter already churned when she opened the pail that night; of the trip across the Mississippi River on a flatboat, with the old grandfather's clock resting on a featherbed that slipped off the flatboat and went floating down the river until it was rescued; of Aunt Til crawling out her window one night and eloping while her "pap" was at home molding bullets to shoot Jim Williamson if he ever came on the place again; and of the winter of the big snow when Papa and one of the Stocker boys were going to Williamson school and the snow was above the high stake-and-rider fence.

Always I was interested in anything about my grandparents. We played with Grandpa's old valise that he took on his annual trips to the mill in Keosauqua. On the flap of one of the partitions was written a list of things he needed to buy. Nails, salt, soda, and tea were on the list. Maybe there were a few other items. Maybe he used this same list each year.

In those days each farm was nearly self-sufficient. My grandfather raised flax. Grandma spun it and wove it into cloth for sheets and tablecloths and even found time in her busy life to weave two beautiful coverlets, one pink and one white, that were given to her daughters after her death. Grandpa had sheep, too. Papa hated them. They had to be shut up in the shed every night so the wolves wouldn't get them. But there had to be sheep for they had to have wool. Grandmother carded and spun the wool into yarn for knitting stockings and mittens for her family and for weaving cloth from which she made her dresses and coats, her shawls, and jeans and wamuses for her menfolk. The warp in her rag carpets was woolen yarn. When the carpet was worn out the yarn that had been the warp was made into beautiful rugs, handhooked to a knitted background. When Grandmother was a seventeen-year-old bride she knitted a pair of socks for Grandfather. The first time he put them on he removed them at once, found the scissors, and proceeded to cut off all the knots. Grandma learned to splice the yarn and knit without knots.

If Grandma was busy and didn't have the noon meal started when she saw the men coming in from the field, she hurried and set the table first of all, then built her fire and started the meal. When Grandpa came in and saw the table was set he would go into the front room to his favorite rocking chair and read the paper until she called for him to come and eat.

We had Sunday school at the schoolhouse in the summertime. Almost everybody in the district attended except two or three of the men. We had some good singers. There were several sopranos; Mamma and Laura Van Cleave sang alto; Friday Simpson sang tenor; and Herman Snow led the basses. They learned new songs for Rally Day, when all the Sunday schools in the township met for an all-day program and big dinner, and for our school Christmas tree at the proper time of the year.

When I was seven, Verlin, Cousin Charley, and some of the neighbor boys started to school. Geneva Stocker was the only girl of that age. She had to dress herself as she had a younger brother and sister. She managed to get her shoes on the wrong feet every day, buttoned up on the inside instead of the outside of her thin ankles.

The teacher and the big girls were excited about a good book that they were reading. Of course I wanted to read it. I took it home with me one night and read from it after supper until time to go to bed. My parents had not paid attention to what I was reading; we had an excellent library at school and I often brought home books. Nobody got much sleep that night; I had one nightmare after another. To their horror my parents discovered that I had been reading what they called a "dime novel." I think the name of it was *Maggie Miller.* I never got to finish it but meekly took it back to school the next day. My mother thought any eighteen-year-old schoolteacher should know better than to give such a book to a seven-year-old to read. After that I was always a little afraid to go past the family graveyard on the way after the cows until after Bert's death. I was no longer afraid when he was over there with Papa's parents and little sisters and Uncle Frank and Aunt Lyde's small children, none of whom I had ever known. Now my parents, Uncle Frank and Aunt Lyde, both my brothers, and many other relatives lie there. It is a very peaceful spot.

We were afraid of the gypsies who often camped under the trees along the roadside just west of the mailboxes. Some of their gaily painted wagons were parked in the school yard. It was a nice spot for them to camp, with our cornfield just over the fence. Uncle Frank's and the Barnes's cornfields were across the road to the north. The gypsies' horses fed well on the big ears of corn and the tall grass from the school yard and the shady roadsides.

Sometimes the campers were horse traders with their sorry looking nags, shabby wagons, and harnesses. We stayed away from them, too. But when the "movers" came along, we liked to talk to them and their numerous offspring. They were going to what sounded like exciting far-off places—Missouri, Kansas, Oklahoma, Nebraska, or Colorado—or they might be coming back from there to their former homes in Illinois or some other far-off spot.

Once some men in a top buggy drove past and stopped in front of the schoolhouse. At recess we saw they had put three chunks of sod as a marker at the corner across the road from the schoolhouse, pointing north toward Blakesburg. The big boys changed them, so they pointed to the east. Presently the gypsy wagons came and turned to the east. I felt so sorry for their poor horses with their sore necks toiling over the clay hills on the wrong road.

The first time an automobile passed our schoolhouse the teacher heard it coming over the hills toward Giles's and Aunt Annie Van Cleave's. She told us there was a car coming and we could go outside to see it. Verlin had seen a car once when he was at Albia with Papa, but most of us had never seen a car before. We stood there watching it go up the tree-lined road past our house, across the Red Bridge, and up over the railroad crossing. My brother and I and Tip Wilson's stepdaughter didn't notice that the other children had gone back into the schoolhouse. We stood there talking about the car until the teacher came to the door and reminded us the school day wasn't over yet.

When I was about fourteen the first picture show came to Blakesburg. My brothers and some of the other boys walked down the railroad track to attend the show. They wouldn't allow me to go along. I seldom went anywhere, but that time I was very anxious to go.

As soon as the supper dishes were done, I started upstairs to bed. A visiting uncle asked me to play the phonograph for him. (At our house it was unusual if there wasn't an uncle, a cousin, or some other relative spending a few days with us.) Later a group of neighbors came. Somebody asked how old I was. Then it dawned on me that it was the night before my birthday and I was being surprised. That was why the boys wouldn't let me go to town with them and why my mother had told her brother to ask me to play the phonograph so I wouldn't go upstairs and feel sorry for myself. We had a good time. The older people were telling such interesting stories that we soon stopped playing and listened to them.

"You were lost in the woods once when you were small, weren't you, Bruce?" asked Ila Barnes, the oldest person present.

I hadn't known that. Papa told about it. He was about seven years old. There were no fences yet. He went with Logan Stocker, eight years old, and Loge's big brother Abe, who was twelve, after the cows belonging to the two families. They followed the tracks west past Fullertons and Hulls. At the corner where the Baileys then lived (and where the Center schoolhouse and the Urbana Center Church would be erected much later) they found that the strays had turned north. They went on past Van Cleaves's and finally found the cows more than three miles from home.

They had rounded them up and started back when they met the Rappalee boy riding a horse. He knew that Abe was very much afraid of wolves. "I saw a great big wolf up by Bailey's," he shouted as he rode past them.

Abe took one frightened glance up the road and took off through the woods to the east as fast as his long legs could carry him. The two little boys trailed after him, trying to keep up.

Shortly after daylight the next morning one of the searchers found the three tired, cold, hungry little boys huddled together by a fallen tree. He jumped on a log and his shouts of "Here they be! Here they be!" echoed through the woods. The little boys had heard the searchers calling to them all through the night, but they were so frightened they didn't know the voices were friendly. They were taken to a nearby cabin where they were fed hot biscuits and raspberry preserves. "It was the best food I had ever tasted," said Papa.

When I was eighteen my brother Bert was killed by lightning in Wyoming. He had taken time off from his work as a telegraph operator in order to stake out a claim of 320 acres and to live on it the required three years to "prove up," as it was called, at which time the land would become his own. With his loaded boxcar containing furniture; fence posts; a cow; a work team; Trixie, the spotted riding horse; some hens; a brood sow; and Robin, our pet rooster, he arrived there in March of 1914. Several other Monroe and Appanoose county residents, with their carloads of possessions, rode the same train. Many other friends, relatives, and neighbors had settled there the previous fall. Thirteen months after his arrival, Bert's body was shipped back home for burial in the family cemetery. That fall Papa and I went out to finish building the fences and disposed of the livestock and crops.

At this time newspaper headlines were screaming ALL EU-

ROPE AT WAR. Soon we read of Iowa boys enlisting in the Canadian or English Air Force. One day our cousin Ronald came walking down the railroad track and sadly told us James Norman Hall, our favorite hero, had been shot down and was believed to be dead. (At the end of the war we learned that he had been a prisoner of the Germans.)

By 1916 all the neighbor boys and cousins had cars. Often the road in front of our house would be full of parked cars, leaving only room enough for passing motorists to get through.

As soon as the United States entered the war Verlin wanted to enlist, but he was not old enough to go without parental permission and Papa would not sign the papers so he could go. It was very soon after Bert's death and I was suffering from tuberculosis, a disease that had killed my mother's mother at the age of thirty-five and her small eight-year-old sister. We had had whooping cough one cold winter and measles another winter, which started my illness. Verlin was quite upset because he couldn't go. He wanted to put a big yellow flag with the word slacker on it in our front window. Nearly all the boys and younger men in the neighborhood enlisted or were drafted. A few of them came back; many died of flu in the training camps.

Three boys from the tiny village of Unionville were killed. The only survivors in their company were wounded. Three brothers, Bert's former schoolmates, who used to live in the log cabin on Uncle Frank's 80 acres across the road from us were together throughout the war. The eldest was decorated for bravery. He didn't want to accept because he said he could not have wiped out the machine gun nest without the help of his brothers and other comrades. When the time came for him to go to Washington to be decorated, his pals packed his suitcase and put him on the train by force.

My sister and I spent the summer of 1918 at the home of our aunt in northwestern Nebraska. The dry air and higher altitude healed my tuberculosis. I returned home with a big appetite and proud of the pounds I had gained. Now at last I was well enough to go back to school. I had expected to go to an Iowa college or university but my parents thought, since Nebraska had helped me so much, that I should go there. I offered no objection. It didn't matter where I went so long as I managed to go back to school. I enrolled for as many subjects as I could, took tests in several subjects I had studied at home, and soon began to feel like a student once more. I wrote a poem each week for the *Eagle,* Chadron State

College's newspaper. I wrote sports news for the school paper and
for the Chadron, Omaha, and Lincoln papers.

In August 1922, Dick and I were married. We lived for
five years on the farm that my great-grandfather Kennedy Robinson had homesteaded when many of the relatives from Indiana
came here in 1846. Vaughn was born there in 1924 and Charles in
1926. In 1927 we bought a farm of our own, complete with mortgage, very near the town of Moulton, about halfway between Centerville and Bloomfield.

2

We Move to Appanoose County

This chapter consists of columns written during the years from 1927 to 1934 when we lived on the farm down by Moulton in Appanoose County. They were published in the *Des Moines Tribune* or the *Centerville Iowegian.* As many of my early columns were general commentaries on the times and tended to contain political or economic viewpoints, I have discarded most of them. Those included here are personal experiences involving members of my family or close neighbors. They are not arranged in strict chronological order (my filing system wasn't good enough to keep them straight).

I T O O K my first plane ride yesterday. It wasn't at all like I had thought it would be. I had expected to be afraid. I wasn't. There wasn't anything to be afraid of. I'm not going to try to describe the flight for I've read and heard dozens of descriptions of rides others have taken—yet I climbed into the seat assigned me without the least idea of how thoroughly I was going to enjoy that ride.

If I tried to tell how I felt and what I saw it would be useless. Those who have never been in the air would get no better idea of it than I did when others described flying to me. And the many, many people who fly already know all about it.

But I am going to mention one thing that I have never heard anyone else say anything about. The junk pile back of the barn, broken-down machinery red with rust, heaps of tin cans and broken dishes in backyards, the shell of a fire-gutted building in a city, and the unkempt huts straggling along the edge of town and the city dump are a few of the objects that are unsightly when viewed by passersby but unbelievably hideous when seen from the air.

I wonder what the birds think of some of the untidy farms they fly over? No wonder some groves are so thickly populated with sweet-voiced songsters, while from others nary a chirp is heard. The birds probably have reasoned that where the grass has no opportunity to grow because the ground is so littered with old boards, cast-off boots, iron wheels, rusty wire, ancient sleighs, and wheelless wagons the worms will be half-starved, not half as fat and luscious as the succulent, green produce to be found crawling about on other farms.

I don't blame the birds one bit. And if I were not so lazy I'd go out and help the boss straighten up things before I forget how ugly the broken grain binder and the old lumber thrown down in an untidy heap looked in one barnyard I saw. There are enough blots on the landscape detracting from the beauty of the fields, the long straight roads and railroads, the ponds and streams, the white houses, and red barns that form so pleasing a picture. I want to be sure that there are no disfiguring blots needlessly marring the scenery hereabouts.

JOSEPH, monarch of the cement tank, is no more.

We miss him with his vivid coat of many colors as we watch the remainder of the fish family darting about in the water. Goldie misses him too. In her grief she refuses to leave the shelter of the big rock. Sometimes we catch a glimpse of gold and white, but Goldie does not appear.

None of us knows just how it happened. It may have been the bullfrog. Or the rock. Or possibly a small bare foot trod unknowingly on a bit of moss that concealed our Joseph.

Wednesday morning when we took the horses to the tank to drink, we saw the bullfrog. Immediately an argument ensued. Do bullfrogs eat baby fish? No one knew. Certainly the fish were not afraid of him, but the small boys insisted that he should not be there. Dick consented to remove the intruder. But that was not easily done. One hop took the big green visitor under the large rock in the center of the tank. Dick raised the rock, thereby imperiling the lives of the whole finny tribe who suddenly had taken shelter there. The frog was gone.

We searched and searched. Finally we found him. Flattened out on the bottom of the tank, he was so nearly the color of the surrounding moss that he could hardly be distinguished from it. After having been forcibly ejected, he uttered a few disdainful croaks and hopped off into the garden.

This morning cries for mother brought me to the kitchen door. I beheld two small boys wading in the forbidden waters of the tank, calling to me to come and see how funny Joseph and Jacob looked swimming on their sides. I ran out and found Jacob still gasping, but Joseph already was dead. So were two of the smaller fish. The boys buried Joseph and Jacob in an empty matchbox.

Dick is sure the boys must have stepped on them. The boys insist the frog came back and killed them. I am positive that Dick dropped the rock on them when he put it back. But we are not saying very much about it, for it is too late now. Joseph is dead.

(The boys were right. The frog came back again. More fish were missing. I broke off a good-sized switch from one of the ash trees; using it as a persuader, I coaxed the murderous bullfrog down the lane and for some distance up the road toward Davis County. He hopped along quite briskly. I derived much pleasure from wielding the switch. Evidently Sir Bullfrog didn't enjoy it so much, for he hasn't been seen since.)

P R O B A B L Y many people wiser than I dislike some of the things I like, such as hoeing, canning, cleaning house, cutting corn fodder, living in the country, being in my thirties, dahlias, roses, meals on time, empty houses with flowers still growing in the yards, old furniture, small boys, books, newspaper editorials, astronomy, chickens, dogs, cows, horses, meat or gravy cooked in a cast-iron skillet, waffles, carrots, and spinach.

It is quite likely that others, and I have no quarrel with them, like many of the things I hate, including petunias, cats, children who have been taught that they are cute, grown-ups who try to act kiddish, male or female sissies, superiority complexes, machine hemstitching, tablecloths hemmed on the machine, cows with horns, weedy gardens, dwelling houses painted green, rain on washday, so-called living rooms that are only used for company, and overstuffed davenports. Large women in striped or checked dresses, bad table manners, being flatly contradicted, people who handle books roughly or who lay an open book face down upon a table, people who read over my shoulder, inquisitiveness, concrete walks in front of farm homes, fried parsnips, mashed potatoes, interruptions while ironing, washing milk pails, cleaning muddy overshoes, cooking for visitors who do not come, going to bed, getting up, washing yesterday's dishes, and talking over the telephone.

You will notice the list of dislikes is longer than the list of likes. That is probably because I ran a splinter under my finger-nail just before I sat down to write, the children are taking the "flu," so is their dad, so am I, and it has been snowing all day!

ON E windy afternoon about four years ago I had just finished ironing and had taken six big loaves of bread out of the oven when the plaster in the kitchen began to fall. By the time I had carried the bread and all the clean clothing I had ironed into the dining room, the plaster, laths and all, had fallen from the ceiling.

The kitchen once had had a ceiling made with wide boards such as were used for ceiling many years ago. When I was small our machine shed, which had been my grandmother's kitchen in the days when our house was a country tavern, and the building where we kept the grain binder, the wood, and the coal had ceilings of the same kind of boards. Some twenty years ago the owner of our present home had lathed and plastered the kitchen, simply nailing the laths to the ceiling boards. The combined weight of the laths and plaster had loosened the nails. I had left the south, east, and west doors all open while I was busy with the washing and ironing and the strong wind had completed the task of spoiling my kitchen with its new wallpaper.

I papered the room again, first the ceiling with newspapers and cloth over the wide boards and then the ceiling and walls with regular wallpaper. The plaster on the walls was in good condition, and I thought the room was as good as new again except not quite so warm as if the ceiling had been plastered. But the mice gnawed holes through the paper where there was a crack all around the room at the top of the plastered sidewall. And some snow that had sifted into the attic melted and dripped down, staining the ceiling paper.

We haven't had much of a kitchen since that time. When winter comes we move the stove into the dining room and with the advent of spring move it back to the kitchen again to struggle with the mice. This spring the stove and cabinet still are in the dining room. The dining room will become a kitchen eventually or else the back porch (when, if ever, we get it built) will have to do.

Dick does not like to have all my books in the living room, since the foundations of houses the age of ours are none too secure. So we have some of the books in almost every room of the house. Shelves containing four hundred or five hundred of them are in the dining room. But when the dining room becomes a kitchen where meat is fried and lard is rendered, it is no place for books. We had planned last fall to move the books into the old kitchen as soon as we could build a foundation under it. But farmers' plans, like those of mice and other men, do not always materialize.

The hogs are out and it is time for the mail carrier, but if we ever get the one-time kitchen fixed, I'll tell you about it.

A R O B I N built her nest in the transom above our front door last week. I do not know just what took place, but one morning I found what had once been the partially completed nest strewn upon the porch floor. I swept up the pitiful collection of sticks and grass, sorry to have lost such a congenial neighbor.

There are so many robins about here that I cannot tell one of them from another, but I imagined that the disconsolate little bird that spent almost the whole day sitting on a fence post near the chicken lot was the owner of the nest that had been destroyed. This robin was a picture of dejection. Her feathers were lusterless as though she was too forlorn and discouraged to properly perform her morning toilet.

But she sat on the fence post only one day. The next day I found more sticks, string, and mud upon the porch floor, not the remnants of what had once been a nest but the leftovers, the odds and ends that had been discarded during the process of building a new home. The second nest is almost done. Even I, who could not possibly construct a habitation out of such simple materials, can see that the present abode is much more strongly and carefully constructed than the first one. The proud housewife is busily adding the finishing touches as I write. She peers through the transom at this noisy typewriter, twists about with a great fluttering of wings and scratching of feet to be sure that all is comfortable, and then flies away for another spear of grass that is needed to make the interior complete.

Snowball, the cat, is a prisoner in the chicken house. Even though the doors are shut this cool morning I can hear his protestations. He does not think he is getting a square deal. In fact, the poor fellow did nothing to deserve punishment. He does not understand that his imprisonment is merely a precautionary measure taken to protect him from the temptation of feasting upon some of the sundry young birds now essaying their first flights out in the orchard. In a few days nearly all the first broods of robins, doves, and other smaller birds will be able to care for themselves and Snowball can be turned outside once more.

White Shoes, the other cat, is not so fond of bird flesh as Snowball. Even if she were, she is much too busy admiring three small felines in the loft of the cow shed to bother about catching birds when there are plenty of mice she can get without straying far from her babies. Luckily, the birds will be able to elude her by the time the kittens are large enough that she needs to forage food for them. There are three small robins in the nest above our door, but they are well feathered and are likely to leave us any day.

As for dogs, Foxie, with her four years' experience in the rural regions, is too wise to molest the feathered babies. The boys are trying to watch Fanny who is spending her vacation in the country for the first time, but she did kill the first baby bird she came upon in spite of the piteous cries of a long-legged parent bird who had followed her offspring when it hopped into the farmyard instead of going in the direction of the pond as she had hoped it would. I don't think Fanny will kill any more baby birds. She is learning country ways very rapidly.

It is rather an exciting experience for a dog, after three uneventful years of life on a city lot, to learn that there are such things as cattle, sheep, hogs, and horses and that they will not molest a lady if she refrains from barking and running after them. She already has learned that it is not necessary for one to run when a group of baby pigs approaches, making strange, fearful grunting noises. She has found that it is only necessary to appear dignified and the piglets will not come too close, but that if one flees they are likely to follow. She has learned that ladylike dogs neither run from nor after the calves. She has discovered the delights of following the corn planter and harrow about the field.

Foxie would feel that she were eternally disgraced if she were locked up for a few moments. But Fannie, unused to liberty, makes no objection when she is put to bed in the granary at night and the doors fastened lest she become homesick and start on an eighteen-mile trip ere morning to see her master. It is a good thing we are not acquainted with many city dogs. I am afraid we'd be softhearted enough to ask all of them to spend the summer here instead of in somebody's hot backyard.

The three small robins above the front door are preparing to leave the nest with much awkward fluttering of wings that seem too large for them. They hop upon the side of the nest; then courage fails them and they huddle down together once again. I fear that tomorrow morning the nest will be empty.

THE boys forgot to fasten two of the gates before they went to the field this morning. The hogs opened the yard gate and came rampaging among the flowers but, of course, could not see the gate when I tried to drive them out again. Instead they spied the other gate and went out into the oat field, and I had to spend a half hour chasing them instead of washing the dishes and the cream separator. We had a shower of rain last night, and the oats are getting so tall that it was not a very pleasant task to run after the porkers who did not mind how wet the oats were. In fact, it seemed to me that they hunted the tallest patches to lead me through.

I have never yet heard a farm woman complain that she did not get enough exercise, so I am positive that I am not the only one who does not always do her tasks according to the schedule. If it isn't the hogs, it is always something else. The windmill has to be shut off at the very busiest time of the day or the tank will run over, endangering the lives of the fish who might swim too near the top of the water. Or the horses refuse to come up and keep getting away from the small boys until Mother goes to their assistance. That happened yesterday, and the washing wasn't done until 4 P.M. and some of the clothes had to be brought in before they were dry last night. Or Dad has to have help getting out or putting away some of the machinery. Or any one of a thousand things may happen. There are always salesmen to bother us, or cabbage plants to set out, or grass to cut, or weeds to pull, or the washhouse to clean.

But we have one advantage over our city sisters. We can work at whatever we most want to do. There is always more than can be done, so we choose what to do and what to let go. It wouldn't be possible to do all the work, so if we prefer to work in the garden instead of cleaning out the chicken house, we can find plenty to do with the hoe. And if we happen to be in the mood to do something else, it usually needs to be done. Of course, we get cross when the hogs, or cows, or horses, or the neighbor's red calf, or a persistent salesman delays our work, but it only makes us more anxious to go ahead with it when we have the chance.

IN my haste to write this I dumped a dish of potatoes into the skillet to be fried before slicing them. Because of the difficulty of handling them, each with a spot of hot grease on one side, it took me longer to get out of the kitchen than if I hadn't hurried so much in the first place.

And now there is a great commotion outside. A tiny pig has his head stuck in the gate. His silly mother and all the other pigs are fighting him—either to make him get out or stop squalling. Despite my desire to deliver the hapless bit of pork from his predicament, I'm too much of a coward to go to his assistance. I'm sure his mother wouldn't appreciate it if I did. Maybe she will soon forget about him and then I can extricate him by pushing the head, which he holds up so stubbornly, down an inch or two.

Somehow it consoles me for the frailties of human nature when a dumb beast acts almost as foolish as a human being. Probably other people do just as many senseless things as I do—I know more about my own actions than theirs. And when an animal doesn't act any more intelligent than we do, I think we might as well stop worrying because we do the wrong things so many times. Instead we can be glad that we manage to do the right thing part of the time.

While I was writing this, the squealing and the woof-woofing of the swine stopped. Seeing that his relatives had gone away and left the imprisoned piglet alone I slipped out to the gate, but I didn't stay long. I was on the back porch by the time the mother hog reached the gate—and it didn't take me long, either. Apparently, it is best to accept the matter with philosophy as the swine have done.

The prisoner seems to think that he will have to stay there; and as he is suffering no discomfort, he doesn't appear to mind enduring something he doesn't know how to escape. The other members of his family, yielding to his stubborn determination to remain in such a place, pay no attention to him so long as I stay in the house. Therefore, there is no reason why I shouldn't stay within.

If Sir Piggie decides to lie down to rest he will release himself automatically. If he doesn't, the boss will get him out when he comes. That will not be long; the potatoes are nearly done, and the boss is not often tardy at the table. He says he doesn't like to be told when it is time to awaken and build the fires, but he never minds being ordered to eat a meal.

THE boys are busy farmers these days. In fact, they have more work than they can do. The last two calves haven't been named and the work of naming the kittens is progressing very slowly. After much learned discussion the white one with the long hair has been named Fluffy. The most favored name among those now under consideration for the striped tiger kitty is Spot, although there are no spots on the kitten.

It hardly seems right to me. Back in the days when the naming of the calves, the colts, the kittens, the pet pigs, and chickens was one of the most seriously undertaken tasks for which I shared a responsibility, striped kittens were always named Timmie. The kitten the boys are now trying to name looks just like the Timmie who accidentally landed in the swill pail when he jumped out of the woodbox with the first mouse he ever caught. But I haven't mentioned the name. Even if it met with the approval of the youngsters, which is not likely, it would be of no use to deprive them of the pleasure of hunting and choosing a name by themselves.

The cat that looks like Timmie will probably answer to the name of Spot unless his (or her) masters decide to call him (or her) either Rex or Clarence. These last two names have been borne by two of the kittens on this farm for the last four or five years, regardless of the color, disposition, or sex of the cat so named.

The Clarences have been unlucky in the past. The last one drowned in the swill barrel. The one before froze to death one night after we had broken up the broody hen under the manger in the cow barn. That Clarence had been wont to sleep beneath Biddy's wings, so we did not discourage her broody temperament until it became warm enough that the cat could be comfortable without her to keep him warm. But when warm weather came we shut the hen up, and it turned cold again in a few days. Poor Clarence, forgotten by all of us until it was too late, perished. Likewise, the careers of the Rexes have had abrupt and tragic endings that have discouraged our cat fanciers and made them decide to give our kittens this year brand-new, unheard-of names so difficult to choose.

There is much other work to be done, too, in the play hours that are none too long at this time of the year when the grown-ups demand so much of a youngster's time and help. The wagon and tricycle road out in the barnyard has to be dragged quite often, and the dogs have to be led about or hauled in the wagon at frequent intervals. The new home for the kittens that is under

construction doesn't seem to be going up very rapidly. It looks
to me much the same as it did when it was a box before the
hammering and sawing began. Some of the work has surely been
accomplished, however, for I heard the seven-year-old tell Dick
that the nails were about gone and he would have to get new ones
the next time he went to town. That was rather a surprise to
Dick, for he hadn't yet used any of the last ones he bought. I
suppose children's work is much like that of their elders. If they
keep working away, they finally will get the most important
things done and be ready for others just as momentous.

We get impatient sometimes when the children think they
are too busy at their play to come to their meals. Yet we are not
so different when we think our tasks are so important that we
have no time left for rest or enjoyment. The world would hum on
just as merrily without us, even if no one else took up the work
we are now trying to do. Maybe we have no reason to laugh at
discussions of names for cats, at dragging roads on hands and
knees regardless of the wear and tear on the overalls or the dirt
and dust on the small faces, at building houses for cats that do
not need them, or at small figures plodding through the dust in
the hot summer sun pulling a wagon in which two dogs are riding.

Maybe we do some foolish and unnecessary work ourselves
sometimes.

WE went fishing the other morning. Of course, there was
plenty of work we could have done, but we didn't want
to work. It was the first time we had ever taken to go
fishing, although we often have been tempted when we saw fishermen passing with their poles tied to the side of the car. Or when
we saw a group of barefoot boys hiking across the pasture with
a string of fish proudly slung across the shoulder of the leader.
We reconciled our qualms of conscience with the thought that it
was high time for the boys to learn the delights of fishing. Imagine a country boy who never held a willow pole in his hands while
he eagerly watched the bobbing cord to see if it was going under!
Besides, the corn was still too small to cultivate and the new
porch, which serves as a kitchen, is finished. Why not celebrate?

So as soon as the milking was done, the milk separated and
carried off to the hogs, the beds made up, and the separator and
breakfast dishes washed, we went up over the hill and down the
other side to the creek. Even the robin, who hatched a brood of
young in the nest above our front door this spring, took two or

three days rest before she began remodeling her nest preparatory to taking up her household duties again. We, too, were taking a vacation, although it would last only two or three hours.

Our fishing equipment was not elaborate. Dick purchased the hooks and manufactured the remainder of it. The bait came from the garden. The fish were not at all insulted that we did not have an outlay of expensive paraphernalia. The small stream they live in is visited every spring by fishermen—youthful, grown-up, middle-aged and gray-haired—who sit in shady spots along its banks and get their catch with simple equipment such as country boys have always used for catching fish.

At every bend in the creek there is a pool and in every pool can be found hungry fish; to be sure they are not always hungry enough to bite, but they are always hungry enough to nibble on a humble angleworm. Perhaps if city fishermen had ever visited this stream the catfish, and even the unassuming sunfish, might put on airs and refuse angleworms offered by barefoot boys. But the city folks fish in the river, so our fish knew nothing about their fancy equipment.

The five-year-old didn't have much luck from a grown-up point of view. Every time a fish nibbled at his bait, he immediately tried to land it before it had taken the hook in its mouth. But he didn't mind at all that he didn't catch any fish. He had a good time trying to catch them.

Dick was lucky. He caught the first fish. And I was lucky. I caught the largest one. Everyone else, even five-year-old Charles, insisted that they had had him on their hooks before I did but that he had gotten away. But I had the satisfaction of knowing that I landed him and they didn't.

Seven-year-old Vaughn was lucky, too. He caught a big catfish and was so proud of it that he had to stop fishing and admire it until the rest of us were ready to go home. And we were all lucky, even if callers did come right after dinner and find out that the sweeping hadn't been done. For we had all the fish we could eat for dinner and supper. And we like fish, specially those we catch ourselves.

REENFORCEMENTS have arrived. The army of chinch bugs that devoured our wheat, rye, oats, and barley has been strengthened by new hatches every day. Now we not only have millions of chinch bugs, we have millions of armies of them. The corn, the timothy, and the grasses that they like best are black with bugs. Farmers need fret no more because they have not had the money to paint recently. Houses, barns, and all the other buildings are black with chinch bugs, whether they have been painted white, red, yellow, gray, or not painted at all. When we come in from the garden and fields we empty them from our shoes before entering the house. We crush them beneath our feet as we walk across the kitchen floor. We find some of the bolder spirits happily swimming in the water bucket. A carefree group romps in the butter dish while their more serious-minded brethren are scouting for new cornfields to feed their ever increasing families.

We have plowed, harrowed, and dragged—no small task when it has not rained for four weeks, the plow refuses to stay in the ground, and the clods fill the shoes of the insignificant humans who are trying vainly to stop the coming of the stubborn little foe. We have shooed, swept, sprayed, and used harsh language, but the enemy comes on. Ignoring casualties, a dozen new warriors take the place of every fallen comrade.

WE are putting soybean hay in the barn these days. The hay is heavy; the flies bother old Roger until he wants to go too fast; and the harness, like Roger himself, is getting old. If Dick gets the hayfork too deep, Roger breaks his harness again and I have to call for help to get it fixed or else some other trouble occurs. It seems like slow going when we take up small forkfuls every time, but we finish sooner that way. Putting hay in the barn is like many other things. The man who is going to get rich quick loses what little he had. Work done hurriedly is seldom done well. If we fill the pail too full to save making another trip to the well, part of the water splashes out.

Roger has shared our good times as well as those not so good for these last ten years. He and Topsy hauled our first not-very-heavy wagonload of possessions to the house back in the field where our career as a farm family began. This morning for the first time in his toil-burdened life, old Roger balked. When I tried to get him to pull up a forkful of hay, he decided it was too heavy. Dick tried to lead him, but he still balked. I used the whip we use when we drive the hogs to town, with no results. Dick applied the hog whip energetically. Roger squirmed about, but the tugs never tightened. We both knew the obstinate creature had been pulling much heavier loads, so we stood and looked at each other helplessly. Presently Roger started up of his own accord and triumphantly hoisted the hay into the barn.

I have always entertained the suspicion that those calm people who never seem to be disturbed by anything have their off-moments like some of the rest of us who are not so outwardly placid. It would be difficult to imagine a more sedate being than dependable old Roger, who has always borne his burdens with such quiet resignation. Never in a hurry, from colthood he has always appeared to be fatigued to the nth degree. Yet when night comes he seems no more tired than the other horses that begin the day prancing. I don't know just what his rebellion this morning signifies. Maybe he wasn't ready to start yet and refused to be disturbed until the psychological moment arrived. Perhaps he has gone temperamental, but I don't think so. I think he decided we were making his work too difficult and he responded like some people who are naturally sweet tempered but the stubbornest of the stubborn when they take a notion to defy everything and everybody.

MY last six weeks have been spent in bed with nothing to do but gaze at the cobwebs in the corner and listen to the crash of falling dishes in the kitchen. The news that I shall probably spend the next six weeks in the same manner does not bring me any joy. Although I have often wished—not recently, however—that I might sometime lie down and rest until I was ready to get up, I have a feeling that when I can leave the bed I am not going to wish to spend very many more hours in it. I don't believe I'd even mind washing the separator if I could be up this nice day. That is, I wouldn't mind it very much—there are other tasks I'd rather do. I've found, too, that it is much more difficult to hit the right typewriter keys when one is lying down.

We often read about the queer names of towns, schools, or localities in other states. One might think that Iowa has no odd names. Yet we have a town named What Cheer.

Vaughn and Charles attend Buzzard Roost school. Other schools not far away are Last Chance, Hard Scratch, Brush College, Hedge College, Hazel College, Scattersburg, Pumpkin Vine, and High Note. Then there are the vicinities of Tick Ridge and Pleasant Valley. Can anyone tell me other queer Iowa names?

3

In the Early 1930s

We entered the 1930s when jobs are scarce, we
scanned the skies for rain clouds that failed to come our way, Bruce
was born in September 1932, and Irvin joined us in August 1934.
We made plans to move and before we left there was painting,
paperhanging, building of a chimney, and refinishing of floors and
woodwork to be done in order that all was ready for the coming of
our tenant family. Vaughn and Charles hated to leave their school-
fellows, Raymond Adams, aged eleven, and his six-year-old brother
Elton. We grown-ups, too, would miss our friends and neighbors. It
was a wrench to leave the home that had been ours for seven years,
our big garden, the poultry houses, and the fields and pastures, but
the farm was a bit small for our needs when Vaughn and Charles
would soon be working in the fields and no adjoining farmlands
were for sale. It seemed best to go back to the old neighborhood
where there were several farms for sale and where we would be
available if our parents needed us in their advancing years.

Bruce was about eighteen months old at the time we were doing the painting and papering; he is the baby mentioned in the first
of these columns. The baby mentioned at the end of the chapter is
Irvin, born August 23. At that time his elder brother ceased to be
the baby and became Bruce.

THE oppressed will submit to only a certain amount of tyr-
anny before they turn upon their oppressors. There are
always good-natured people who will undergo unjust treatment for a long time without a murmur. But when they are
aroused—let their tormentors beware!

The big boys (eight and eleven years old, respectively) in our
school readily admit that they are greatly superior to the little

boys who are only six. Small boys understand that a boy a few years older is to be greatly admired. They know that it is their duty to serve in the capacity of errand boys and to be cheerful about it. They are rather proud to be noticed at all. They do not object to being disdainfully cuffed about and made to keep their proper places. They understand that it is the right of those superior beings whom they serve and admire to get the first drink, the biggest apple, and the best playthings. They do not mind using books that were purchased for an elder brother or the short pencils that he has cast aside scornfully. They offer no objections to wearing big brother's outgrown overalls with the patched knees while the big boys get all the new clothes.

Being the mother of a big boy and also a small one I trust that I can view what has happened in a wholly impartial manner. To me the big boy, in spite of his eight years, seems hardly grown up. I try to let them fight their own battles without reprimanding the victor to deprive him of some of the joy of winning. Small boys delight in playing the part of flunky to a supercilious big boy if grown-ups do not interfere. And there is nothing so despicable as the whiney tattletale whose parents force the big boys to baby him because he is the littlest.

The six-year-olds have not complained because they are the ones who have to be "it" in playing games at school. If they have felt their treatment has been unjustly burdensome at times they have kept their thoughts to themselves, for no one has heard them murmur. Charles and Elton are only second graders and do not expect any deference. This thing of going to school is so wonderful a privilege that they are glad to undergo some humiliation rather than to play lonesomely at home as they did when they were four. But when Vaughn and Raymond went in the coal house and held the door shut as the climax of a series of indignities it was too great an insult. Even second graders cannot ignore such gross insolence. Revenge was in order. There is a lock on the coal house door, but they didn't think of locking it and jailing the tyrants. They merely gathered a supply of ammunition in the form of small pieces of coal that were scattered about on the ground. Like old campaigners they lay in wait for the enemy to appear.

When the big boys discovered that nobody was trying to get in, the coal house no longer appeared attractive. They emerged to meet a shower of missiles. Rapid firing made up for poor aim. It was impossible to miss every time. Vaughn received a jagged chunk of coal in his right eye. The battle ended then and there.

A scared group ran to the schoolhouse for first aid. The wounded soldier had closed his eyes, and thus saved his eyesight. His eyelid was cut through and will always bear a jagged scar.

The small boys have won one engagement. Victory is sweet. They are sorry the enemy had to be punished so severely, but both of them claim the honor of being the one to inflict the wound. It is my guess that their days of oppression are about ended and that they will soon be admitted to the ranks of the big boys.

WHEN winter arrived and it became necessary for the youngest member of the family to spend much of his time in the house, we moved the living room table in front of the bookshelves. We reasoned it was easier to make it impossible for a small boy to reach the books than to break him of the habit if he should begin taking them out of the shelves.

But it was easy for him to move the chairs around. Although not sure which direction the chair would go, by perseverance and keeping his temper Bruce managed to get a chair close enough to the table to climb upon it every time he was left alone in the room. When he stood up on the table and threw the books to the floor, they made a dandy noise. When he heard footsteps it was an easy matter to slip to the floor quickly. Although it hurt terribly when his head hit the floor, a few tears soon stopped the pain.

We moved the table. We did not know how we were going to save the books. If all those bumps from falling off a table several times a day could not teach him to leave them alone, it was hardly worthwhile to depend upon whippings to have any effect. At any rate the unprotected books would not have so far to fall if the thrower had to stand on the floor. But we had no more difficulty. Books that are easy to get at are no longer tempting. Once more the uncomplaining rubber cat, the wooden engine, and the blocks are the center of interest.

One of our horses has a habit of reaching over the fence to eat the grass in the hog lot. The wire sags, the posts lean, and it is a never ending task to replace missing staples. One day the horses had to be shut up in the hog lot. At last the big black had an opportunity to eat the grass she had been wanting all summer. We watched. She went to the fence and, reaching over, began to graze on the other side of the wire—in the horse pasture.

The boys and girls who make themselves look silly by aping

grown-ups grow into the men and women who ridiculously imagine everyone thinks they are youthful and cute. The farmer's son goes to town and becomes a lawyer, doctor, clerk, mechanic, or street sweeper and spends the remainder of his life wishing he had stayed on the farm. The town youth determines to become a gentleman farmer. He becomes a landowner and lives in his car either on his way to town or back home for meals.

All my life I have wanted to write. You can't imagine how glad I am that I have this article done and won't have to worry about writing another one for a day or two.

WE have tried to teach the children to keep their toys picked up and put away except when they are playing with them. Sometimes they forget but they do quite well most of the time, considering how busy they are at work and play during all their waking hours.

My sister doesn't see my children very often, so she doesn't know how particular they are about the matter. She was quite surprised the other day when she came into the living room to find the half-completed jigsaw puzzle, on which she had worked nearly half a day, neatly packed away in its box. Her nephews explained they were afraid someone might bump against it, knock it over, and thus lose some of the tiny pieces.

WE have enameled the woodwork in the living room and are ready to begin putting on the wallpaper. I am writing at a desk on which rests a clock, thirty-one strips of sidewall, four long strips of border, an oilcan, one of the Christmas games, a can of nails, the sewing box, a mail-order catalog, a linen picture book, two school notebooks, three handkerchiefs, a glove, a knife, a spoon, and a rock one of the boys admires and treasures. The sewing machine and my dresser are piled high with books. I wish I could find my hairpins and comb. The refrigerator is loaded with vases, lamps, hats, and the scraps of wallpaper. The kitchen cabinet, worktable, and stove are almost hidden under an assortment of articles.

There is a paintbrush and a pan of paste in the sink. The ceiling paper is on the dining table on a protecting layer of newspapers, cut and ready to be pasted. The kitchen tables are in the living room. We'll stand on them to put on the paper. Where and what we shall eat when mealtime comes is a question that will have to be answered later. I'm too busy to think about such trivial matters at present.

The baby has enamel on his hands and paste in his hair. Enthusiastically two very dirty "big" boys are tearing off the last bit of the old wall covering. It's too bad to neglect the dog and the kittens so shamefully. But when so much of interest is going on indoors it is impossible for Vaughn and Charles to find time to play with cats. The felines will have to find some method of entertaining themselves for a day or two.

O N our front porch is a little fox terrier. She has no pedigree. Her ancestors were ordinary dogs. I do not know that any of them had pedigrees. Probably among them were some of the nobility and others who were very, very plebeian. Just like your ancestors, and mine. But Foxy is the cleanest dog I ever saw. Even when it is raining she keeps the mud from her white coat. She is an aristocrat in her tastes. She eats from a clean pan or she does not eat. If another dog or a nasty cat tastes her breakfast the meal is ruined for her. She thinks her folks are the best people on earth and refuses to allow other people in the yard if her folks are gone. She hates dirty tramps and the neighbors' livestock.

Just outside the back gate, seven puppies are romping. They have the bluest of blue blood in their veins. Their ancestors came from England and have pedigrees with high sounding names. But they do not conduct themselves as one would believe the scions of nobility would act. They take unfair advantage of one another, grasping a tender ear and shaking it with all their might in spite of the howling protests of the poor victim. They wade through every mud puddle and care not for their appearance. They eat greedily and, I'm ashamed to say, noisily—so noisily that Foxy goes back to the house in disgust. They even play with the silly cats that Foxy will not condescend to notice. They are as glad to see visitors as if they were the equals of the folks who live here. They know no better, but Foxy does.

Of course, the puppies will be the best hunters. Foxy wouldn't think of going into the water after a duck that had just been shot. She might get her feet muddy along the riverbank. She does not mind working, but it must be at tasks where her dignity will not suffer. Since she is one of the commoners and the spaniels are of the upper class one would think that they would be the ones who were careful to uphold their poise on all occasions.

But I do not believe that noble ancestry will make us ladies and gentlemen any more than I think that we are doomed if some of our progenitors were cowards or rascals. One of the silliest things we can do is to judge ourselves or others by our ancestry.

T H E chore boys are gone on a short vacation. Things are quiet, too quiet, around here. Small brother stays in the house most of the time. There isn't much fun playing with the dog and the cat without Vaughn and Charles to help. The pup worries the kittens awhile and then comes back to lie on the porch where she can watch the door in hope that someone will come out and talk to her. Not only little brother, the dog, and the kittens think this is a lonesome empty life without our two rollicksome noisemakers; Daddy and Mother find little to say. The newspapers are not interesting. I wonder if it could have been this quiet back in those days when there were no boys at our house?

It will not be long until school begins, and then five days a week will be lonely ones. It helps a lot to go into the north bedroom at nights and see two lads there safe asleep even though they have been gone all day. The last few days have made us realize how many steps our helpers save us. Now there is no one to run to the shop for the hammer and a few sixes or eights. No one brings me a fresh drink every little while. Frequently I take small sips of the tepid water that is left from our noon meal, but it does not quench the thirst like cold water from the well. I have to hunt the eggs, dig the potatoes or do without, water the flowers, and go to the basement after the cream and butter. There isn't anyone to go to the mailbox, feed the chickens, bring up the cows and horses, wash and dry the dishes, and look after the youngest member of the family.

Grown-ups think it would be nice to be young and carefree again with long, long days for play, but when they begin to do all the little tasks that interrupt a farm child's play, they wonder that small lads and lassies are not too tired for games and make-believe when they do have a few free moments.

It is good for children to have a gala week or two away from home. They need rest from the tiresome chores. It is good for them to see strange sights and learn things that are new to them. When they return, home and home tasks look good to them. It is good for parents, too. Sometimes they are inclined to think that their task of clothing, feeding, training, and caring for the

family is one that brings no thanks. They forget that they are
receiving just as much as they are giving. When the small travelers return their efforts will be better appreciated and their mistakes more easily overlooked.

Of course, we expect children to be perfect in every particular.
All big folks do. Adults are not perfect. They spill things, drop
perishables, and forget important matters, but they have so much
more to distract them than little people do. That is what we
think—until we try to do the children's work for a short time.
Then we begin to wonder if it isn't pretty much of an advantage
to be a grown-up?

TO those who have inquired about the omission of the farm
woman's column recently: I lost my father seven weeks ago.
Any of you who have given up a parent will understand
why I lost interest in my work. The end was sudden. We were
away from home for a night and a day and my people were unable
to locate us, so I did not hear of his death for several hours. It
has been hard to realize that Dad and I will never work in the
fields again or drive old June up to the other place to salt the
cattle. It has been hard to go back home again when he is not
there.

It was getting late. We could not hope to reach home in time
to do the chores before dark. If we managed to water the flowers,
hunt eggs, and turn the livestock into the lot to drink we'd have
to be satisfied. We would have to do the milking and other chores
by lantern light.

As we rounded a corner a terrific "Bang!" made everybody
except the sleeping two-year-old jump.

"Backfire," I remarked hopefully, although I didn't believe
it.

"Muffler blew off," quoth nine-year-old Vaughn, wise in the
ways of motors and other mysterious machinery that ignorant
woman can not hope to understand.

"Do you think it was. . .?" groaned the driver, as he brought
the car to an abrupt stop.

"I'm afraid it was," I said, as he climbed out to inspect the
rear tires. We hadn't had a blowout for three or four years. It
couldn't happen to us tonight of all nights, when we needed to
hurry. But it had happened. There was a great slit in an almost
new casing, a bigger one in the inner tube.

Vaughn and Charles scrambled out of the car to help. It wasn't easy, for we were packed well with every inch of space in use. In addition to the five people, a suitcase, and some packages that occupied the seats, we had another passenger. Her position was not at all comfortable. She was moaning and panting because she was hot and the ropes hurt her. There isn't a great amount of room between the seats of our car for a Jersey calf almost half a year old.

Luckily our forced stop was in a village, so there would not be a long walk to find a jack we could borrow. (Our own hadn't been of much use since the truck driver borrowed it the day he broke his truck. With its help he had managed to get the truck to the city where he traded it for a new one, but there wasn't much left of the jack.)

Whew! It was a hot corner. I opened the doors to make it a little cooler for the suffering calf. Passing cars threw dust on us contemptuously. Some men riding in a roadster looked at us, at each other, and grinned. It looks funny to see someone else sweating over a tire pump. It seems a bit foolish of the other fellow to have allowed a tire to blow out. We knew what they were thinking, but we didn't blame them. We felt a bit silly ourselves. The roadster swerved back into the street in front of us as soon as it was safely past. There was a loud explosion, the rattle of a fender as something struck it, and the machine skidded crazily to a stop a few feet in front of us.

The occupants climbed out and grinned at us again. Not superior grins this time, just brotherly ones that acknowledged us to be comrades in misfortune. I guess most drivers have tire trouble occasionally.

THE well-dressed, glib-tongued salesman of a few years ago was no problem. It was fun to get rid of him quickly, without allowing him to know that one really wanted but didn't need what he was selling and there was money in the family pocketbook to pay for it. That the money in the purse was to be spent for something else or to be put in the savings account would not have mattered to the sleekly groomed, smooth-talking agent. He liked to convince people that they needed his product more than any necessity of life.

The experienced salesman isn't the only man who knocks at our door now. The shabby young men who nervously shift from one foot to the other while they try to remember the sales talk they had practiced at home are not so easily dismissed as their more capable fellow-workers. It is no fun to argue with them. The poor kids are discouraged so easily. They are only half convinced that they can learn to sell anything. However, it is impossible to buy from all of them, no matter how badly one feels when one is turned away. They are willing to barter, but we do not have something to trade every time. They have taken the white elephants of the household in exchange for what they are selling, and now we have another collection of useless articles in the attic.

After one has made a purchase the would-be salesman is not so tongue-tied. He brags about his wife and baby that are staying with "her folks" up at Tama or over at Keokuk or down at Mount Ayr. It is much easier for a homesick lad to talk about his family than to describe the merits of the wonderful invention he is trying to sell.

Every day a different little car, sometimes coughing or rattling pathetically, drives up our cinder path. With firmness I repeat that we have no money, hens, or potatoes to trade and that we do not need the contrivance or the magazine. If the stranger puts up a good line of talk, if he boasts that he sold at every house he stopped at yesterday, he is sent on speedily. Some of them, disappointed but not surprised, leave at once and dispiritedly drive up the road. Others, according to their various natures, stay to argue or to plead.

One Monday I refused to buy from one of them. As he started down the steps he said he was hoping to sell here, for there was no washing on the line. Everywhere he had found the housewives washing and too busy to talk to him. I replied that I would have been washing, too, if the baby had been feeling better.

"Say, listen," the shabby youth came back to the door. "Our baby is sick sometimes and my wife doesn't get anything done but take care of her. Have you got your housework done? Couldn't I do the sweeping and wash your dishes for something to eat?"

What did I do? Well, what would you have done? The bread was not ready to bake, so I couldn't feed him, but I bought his magazines and he went back to town to buy his dinner. I told him he needn't do any housework. I was sure I would get it done later.

And then there was the lad who wanted to trade for my Bible. When I found another one for him, he had to sit on the steps and admire it for a long time. I helped him find the blank pages in which to write a family record. I learned that he was a proud husband and father; that he had not gone to high school but had stayed at home to help his father, who had finally lost the farm after all; and that he had made two dollars the previous week after having paid expenses. I heard many other things that the boy far from home finds easier to talk about than the product he is trying to sell.

One chap timidly asked if I cared if he looked at the sample copy of "How to Sell" that came in the mail the other day. I gave it to him. I didn't need it. What I need is a volume telling "How to Keep from Buying."

SO M E people can do their sweeping and dusting on Friday or Saturday and the house stays clean until the next weekly cleaning day. But it isn't that way at our house. Our living room, dining room, and kitchen have to be cleaned at least once a day. There are more days when the sweeping is done two or more times than there are when it doesn't have to be done at all. There are toys, bits of paper, string, cardboard, crayons, dominoes, checkers, and various other possessions of the schoolboys that must be picked up before the sweeping is begun. Sometimes the owners pick them up and other times they forget and go to school, leaving it all for Mother to do.

The porches are all tracked up and have to be scrubbed every day. There is a big washing to do once or twice a week. Patches are required on overall knees and shirt sleeves. Cuffs get frayed from repeated rubbing on the washboard and have to be replaced with new ones. Bread has to be baked two or three times a week. Windowpanes are washed weekly, yet they always bear the marks of small fingers. Faces and hands will not stay clean. Shoes come untied. Tousled hair needs combing. Pencils and books get lost. The play gets most boisterous about the time the baby goes to sleep.

A red-wheeled wagon and a wobbly tricycle have worn a path around the house until the grass will no longer grow there. A homemade scraper and road grader (I know that is what they are because the boy who made them told me) recently made a new road through my favorite flower bed. Gates sway drunkenly because they have been swung upon too often. Shrubs are broken off during the excitement of hide-and-go-seek games. The front lawn is untidy because too much time is spent cooking, washing, ironing, mending, and dusting. By the time these tasks are over it is time to begin again, and so the yard gets very little attention. Sometimes the dusting and the ironing are not done at all.

Company always comes before the house is cleaned or while the unwashed breakfast dishes are still on the table.

But two lads are ever ready to run to the basement or the attic for something for Mother. She has a fresh drink whenever she asks for it. She never has to dry the dishes. She has help in the garden in summer. She used to have to go after the cows, but now they are brought up the lane in half the time it used to take her to get them. There doesn't seem to be much work for her to do in the fields nor at chore time any more, for there is always a boy or two to drive the team or feed the calves or water the chickens.

Her culinary efforts are appreciated. She is told that she is the best cook in the world. She knows that she isn't, although they do not. They like what she cooks, and so long as flattery is sincere it is not to be despised. Stormy Sundays are no longer lonesome days. Sundays in winter used to be long, long days— now they are far too short. I'm glad I am not one of those housekeepers who only has to sweep the room once a week.

THE other members of the family are quite busy painting the house this week. The two youngest lads have no paintbrushes, but they are just as busy as the painters. They have almost as much paint on themselves as there is on the house. I cannot open a screen door, pick up the broom, or grasp the pump handle without getting white paint on my hands. On one end of the kitchen cabinet, newly enameled a short time ago, is the white print of a small hand. I discovered the fingerprints on the dining table in time to remove them before they dried.

My caustic comments do no good. I doubt if they are heard at all, for the boys are too occupied to pay much attention to a mere female who cannot be expected to know anything about painting. When boys are seven and not quite two they can get quite a thrill out of running about and getting in everyone's way if nothing better offers itself to be done. At any rate the two I know can.

As for nine-year-old Vaughn, he is quite an important personage since he has been deemed old enough to wield a paintbrush. He feels quite grown-up as he mounts the tall, shaky ladder and climbs from it to the high scaffold at the gable end of the house. But when that portion of the painting is finished and it is time to descend from the scaffold he is just a scared little boy. He may be only ten or twelve feet from the ground, but it looks like a long distance to him. He clings tightly to the planks with both hands as he feels about for the ladder with his feet. No one seems to notice if his voice trembles a bit as he orders Charles to hold the ladder firmly so it will not slip. This isn't just like climbing trees or the windmill. Once off the scaffold Vaughn regains his confidence and comes down the ladder jauntily, aware of the envy of Charles who thinks painting would be more fun than taking care of the baby.

Knowing that I do not count in a time like this, I do not voice my fears. I only hope no one will get hurt. And that the paint-bedaubed flowers in the window boxes will not die. I go back into the house after one more look at the much trampled shrubbery that I have tended so carefully. It looks pretty sick now, and how will it look by the time the house gets a second coat of paint? It doesn't take much to discourage growing things when the ground is so dry. Nor does it take much to discourage the one who is trying to grow them.

Well, I wanted the house painted, didn't I?

A L M O S T any mother whose children are grown can tell you that modern mothers do not know much about child-rearing and the training of future citizens.

She had no difficulty with hers. They were content to lie upon the floor or to sit in the highchair and play with whatever was given them. They did not get into things. They never, never broke their playthings. They did not quarrel. They fed themselves without getting cereal on their dress fronts or egg in their eyebrows. They dropped no crumbs and spilled no milk upon the floor. When one of them became sleepy, it went to sleep with a toy in one hand and a contented smile on its face even if the mother was busy in the kitchen or garden. All the competent parent had to do was to carry it to its own little bed. In an hour or two it came out of the bedroom rosy and smiling.

(Excuse the fifteen-minute interruption. I had to stop and rock the baby.)

As I was saying, babies of fifteen or twenty or forty or fifty years ago were not much bother. To be sure, the washings were somewhat larger right at first, but after the first year hardly enough to mention. Little girls required one or two clean dresses each week and boys a like number of shirts and overalls. They didn't tear them, either. Nor did they get into the axle grease or wear holes in the knees of their stockings. Some of the neighbors' kids did such things, but then one could not expect much else from such an outfit.

In those days children did not kick up the rugs, leave torn paper on the floor, or track in dust and dirt. Toys were kept in a playbox or on a shelf designed for that purpose. They did not swing on gates or leave them open so the chickens could get into the yard or garden. They helped to take care of the baby chicks. They loved to hoe in the garden. The little ones pulled weeds as soon as they were old enough to walk. Even the tiniest one did not need to be told to wash before meals and at bedtime. They washed clean, too, and did not leave dirty streaks on the towel. They learned to wash their own necks and ears at, what seems to mothers of today, an amazingly early age. Each kept its handkerchief in its own small pocket and wiped its nose without prompting. By the time they were old enough to go to school they were very particular about keeping their fingernails filed and immaculate.

Small boys were quite fussy about their hair. It was kept slicked back from morning until night. If an unruly lock crept out of place, the youngster took his comb out of his pocket and tidied it up.

I guess they put it over the kids of today, all right. They must have been a drab, uninteresting lot. The four boys who keep things pepped up around here are quite different. But I'll have to go. The baby is waking and wants to be rocked.

4

We Move and Build a House

In the fall of 1934 we left the farm down by Moulton and moved back to Monroe County. While we were building our new house at the top of the hill, we lived for a few months in an old log cabin. The columns in this chapter deal with life in the cabin and the joys and problems of building our new house.

A L L my life I have thought it would be wonderful to live in a log cabin as our ancestors did. We have been living in one for the last six weeks. And I'm satisfied. The urge to revert to the primitive has disappeared. Although there are seven of us and our cabin has three rooms, I am sure we feel quite as crowded as did the pioneers when twice as many people lived in one or two rooms.

The workmen have started our new house. It can't be finished too soon to suit me. A few cold days and nights have discouraged the flies that have been pouring in at our screenless doors and windows. But the flies were not the only ones discouraged by the icy mornings. It isn't much fun to get breakfast in a kitchen when the cold wind drifts up through the cracks and knotholes in the worn floor. I miss the furnace at such times.

I just wonder if our renters appreciate that cistern pump at the kitchen sink? And the well just outside the yard fence? I can remember complaining because I had to go through a gate every time I went after a bucket of water. Our ten-gallon cream cans are no longer new and shiny; we use them to hold the drinking water that we haul from Grandma's house three miles away. On washdays we heat the water in the teakettle and my large pre-

serving kettles. The washboiler and tub are kept full of soft
water—if it rains often enough. On rainy days every crock, jar,
pan, and bucket is set under the eaves to catch the rainwater.
Sometimes the washing has to be done by hand because there
isn't enough water to use the machine. There is a well near our
back door, but the water is too hard to use for washing and we
do not like it for drinking.

Other things make it quite unhandy to live in a house that
has been unoccupied for years. There are no outbuildings unless
you count the brooder house that we brought with us to house
a few speckled hens. I miss the washhouse, barn, and granaries,
which I had taken for granted. It isn't much fun to milk outside
in the rain. The kitchen has to serve several other purposes in
addition to being the room where our meals are prepared. Besides the kitchen and dining room furniture, it contains a wardrobe from one of the bedrooms, the refrigerator, washing machine,
and numerous trunks and boxes. Our coats and various everyday
garments are hung on nails driven in the log walls by our predecessors. Our better clothes are kept in dresser drawers. If we
know it in time before we "go places" we press them. If we do not
have time for that, we wear them full of wrinkles.

I might write of many other things that we have found
different from living in a more modern house. I'll have to admit
that I've cheated sometimes. No pioneer woman ever sprayed the
flies to kill them. She brushed them out with a maple branch. She
didn't have a washing machine or sewing machine either. But
this life is primitive enough to suit me. I'm quite satisfied.

M E N make fun of women for moving the furniture around
so often. Until recently I didn't know why it was impossible for me to live happily for more than a week without
taking a bed upstairs or bringing a rug or chair down. At last I
know. I've learned why it is just as natural for a woman to change
the location of the sofa and tables every few days as it is for a dog
to bury a bone or for the squirrel to cache some of his acorns in
the corner of his cage.

The ancestors of the dog and the squirrel had to store supplies for future use when no food was available. Their descendants inherited the instinct. Womankind has inherited the instinct
to shove the bed over in the southeast corner of the room one
week and back to the middle of the north wall the next.

A few generations ago there were many tiny homes housing

large families. There were no unnecessary articles of furniture in those houses. Even with only the essential chairs, table, beds, cupboards, and wardrobes there was no waste space. The only way the housekeeper could clean the floor was to put the chairs on the table and beds, sweep the space thus left in the middle of the room, move one article of furniture to the space, clean the place where it had been, put another piece of furniture there, etc. When all was finished the article in the middle of the room was moved into the last place swept.

It sounds quite simple, but it is much easier to clean a house of eight or ten rooms than one that contains only the bedroom and kitchen. I know. We lived in three rooms for two months this fall. Since cold weather came, we have been living in one room. The other two rooms are so cold we can't heat them with the one small stove we have. I have just finished sweeping our combination living room, kitchen, dining room, pantry, bedroom, nursery, and bath. I moved eight pieces of furniture, not counting the boxes that take up all the space under the bed or the chairs.

When I moved my desk the clock upon it stopped, and after I finished sweeping I had to call a neighbor to find out the time of day. (I suppose clocks used to stop before there were telephones. By referring to the almanac the housewife could set the clock at sunrise or sunset. But I wonder what she did on cloudy days?)

If my great-great-granddaughters are prone to spend much time rearranging their household treasures, it will be because they inherited the instinct from one of their foremothers who back in 1934 spent many hours juggling beds, tables, and cupboards in a futile attempt to rout her enemies, Dust and Dirt.

WE have a Christmas tree up in the kitchen of the log cabin where we are staying while the new house is being built on the hill. It is only a branch of a cedar tree, broken off by the heavy snow. The trimmings are some the boys made from scraps of paper the teacher had left over after they decorated the tree at school. There wasn't room for it on the floor, so they put it on top of the boxes of books that are piled across one side of the room.

However it is a real Christmas tree, and three small lads are very proud of it. They showed it to the baby and explained all about the gifts. He isn't much interested—Irvin doesn't know about Santa Claus yet—but he feels quite flattered when the three big boys all talk to him at once. Children have to have Christmas even though there isn't much room for Christmas trees. The biggest day in the year must be gay for them.

The big folks cannot feel the same about the holiday season since the family circle is no longer intact. In spite of ourselves our thoughts dwell on that Christmas day a year ago, which was the last time we saw the one who preceded us on the long journey. But we need not remind the little folks that there is no happiness in our hearts. Dad had his sorrows and troubles when he was alive, but he did not allow them to interfere with our happy times. He wouldn't want us to spoil the pleasures of his beloved grandchildren just because he cannot be here to enjoy Yuletide with them.

At the other grandpa's house there will be no empty chairs. There will be three new grandbabies to enjoy their first Christmas gifts. Only three of all the grandchildren have two grandfathers now, for I am not the only one of the in-laws who has known real grief since the last of the family gatherings. May we have the strength to hide our melancholy and join the merrymakers.

We have had so many jolly Christmases to remember. We would not rob our little ones of one shred of the happiness that is due them.

UNPACKING the trunks and boxes and getting settled in a new house doesn't appeal to the baby, who feels that he is neglected unduly. But it is an interesting task for boys of two, eight, and ten years. Even mothers and daddies well up in the thirties get quite a thrill out of it when it is the first new house they have ever owned.

Two-year-old Bruce likes to dress up. Every time one of his suits was unpacked he insisted that he needed a clean one. Finally he discovered one of his favorites that he had not worn since last summer. He started to don it at once. A maternal warning that it was too cold a suit to wear on such a chilly day received an understanding grunt. The fat arms that had been thrust into one sleeve and one leg of the garment were withdrawn and the small helper trotted out of the room. In a moment he reappeared with the announcement, "Suit warm now." It was plenty warm, for it was blazing. He had held it up before the open fire because I had told him it was too cold when I meant to tell him it was made of lightweight material that would not keep him warm in winter. It is so easy to be misunderstood when we say what we mean. It is easier still when we make an ambiguous statement and expect our listeners to translate it into what we had intended to say.

A written message or a telephone conversation is less likely to be lucid than spoken words. And millions of quarrels have started and millions of enemies have been made because somebody said something, in all innocence, that somebody else took as an insult. We know that it is our habit to speak slovenly and that listeners are apt to be inattentive and get things wrong even if we are careful. But we often make no effort to improve our choice of words or to give more attention to what others say. If we talked less and were sure that the words we uttered conveyed our meaning; if we listened more closely and made sure that we did not misinterpret the statements of others when they were merely speaking clumsily and thoughtlessly instead of sarcastically or bitterly; and if we made an extra effort to choose our words well when writing letters or talking on the telephone, we'd be able to spare ourselves the greater part of our troubles.

Things that were not said and things that never happened cause more people to lose their tempers than all else put together. Grown-ups don't shed tears every time they get a minor injury. It's funny they can't grow up in other ways, too.

W E have been laying flooring.
I have remarked several times that putting paper on the wall is quite a task. I used to think it was slow work to shell peas to can. On washdays when I had to bake bread, churn, and cook for hands I thought I was quite busy, especially if the babies were fussy. Trying to make a pig or a cow go back through the same hole in the pasture fence that it escaped from isn't the easiest thing in the world to do. Keeping the neighbors from discovering something you do not want them to know is almost impossible. Teaching a bunch of pullets to roost in the laying house instead of in a cherry tree has caused many a flock owner to lose both her temper and her desire to raise chickens. Melting enough snow to make a boiler full of water on washdays is tedious work. Arriving in a strange town just in time to see your train leave is provoking, especially when no other train is due for twenty-four hours—the long wait in a dingy, uninteresting railway station or hotel is not restful and the hours seem like days. Few women like to wash a churn or cream separator. Some of them complain when they have to clean mud off the floors. Oth-

ers object to washing greasy overalls. Few men like to change a
flat tire or put on chains. Small boys and some small girls dislike
to wash before meals. Most of us hate to go to bed and hate to
get up.

Any of these tasks is a mere chore compared to the one of
cutting, fitting, and nailing an oak floor to native two by eights.
When the nail doesn't bend or the flooring split, the amateur
carpenter manages to hit his thumb just to make things interesting.

So after spending two or three days helping with the floor I
am not minding the task of moving as much as I did the other
two times we changed our dwelling place. Both babies are cross
today because we are trying to pack our possessions. The two-
year-old is doing a share of the packing, but the trouble is that
he packs things we do not want packed and unpacks boxes we
have ready to go. We are planning to move into the four basement rooms to live until the rest of the house is finished. In order
to be more comfortable we intend to take only the things we
need, for we are getting tired of being so crowded. It is necessary
to decide which articles need be taken and which are nonessen-
tials that may be left for a while.

There isn't much time to think because there is dinner to
prepare, bread to bake, the baby to rock, and the next-to-the-
baby to subdue so we can move directly after the noon meal. But
oddly enough I can't worry a whole lot about the difficulties of
today. I'm fretting about how long it is going to take to floor the
other five rooms when we had such a time getting only the kitch-
en and dining room floored.

D I C K drives nails one day, that is, after the milking, separating, and feeding are done; and then hauls wood, repairs
fence, and hauls feed or bedding for three or four days.
Sometimes he has to take the team and wagon to town for lumber
or other supplies. Again he yields to the temptation to lay some
more flooring in the haymow or do some other long neglected
work at the partly finished barn. When the ground is not frozen
too hard and it is not too muddy he works with the horses and
scraper trying to grade the lawn and barnyard so they will drain
better. The time taken to clean out the well is not to be regretted,
for the bothersome task of hauling water has been eliminated.
The wood sawing took many days, but now it isn't necessary to
chop wood every day. Putting in the stanchions for the milk cows

was another time-saver. Cows that have been milked in stanchions for years can get quite contrary when one tries to milk them out in the pasture.

But even though I have to be satisfied if one short day a week is spent at the house I suppose it will be finished someday. The roads haven't been any too good for bringing out building materials. Our native walnut that we are going to use for the finishing work is not quite cured, so I have to try to be patient.

It sounds easy, but it is much easier to talk about patience than to practice it. When we need some of our belongings that have been packed away since last summer, we are not sure where to find them. They are likely to be at any of the homes of the six neighbors and relatives who have made room for the things we couldn't keep here.

In spite of all the inconveniences that annoy us at times, it is quite handy to be here where we can work at the building whenever we have a day or an hour to spare. I needn't worry about whether the work is being done as I want when I am here to supervise. I needn't go off and leave the babies when I need to decide some momentous (to us) question about the location of a window or a cupboard. It is much easier to know just how we want each room arranged when we are living in it than it would be if we were living somewhere else and looking at a plan on paper. So I guess if we ever build another house (and it makes my head ache just to think about it) we'll live in it just as soon as the roof is on the building.

U N L I K E the rest of the state, we have not had much ice to bother us this winter. There has been plenty of it on the creeks and ponds, but it hasn't been out of bounds until recently. Our roads, fields, lawns, and walks were a glare of ice for a few days. We can understand now why our neighbors north of us have been objecting to so much skating this winter. Skating is all right for those who like it, but it is a bit unreasonable to expect everybody to want to skate all the time.

Much to my surprise I haven't fallen down. Although the other members of the family (with the exception of the two youngest who have been kept indoors) have managed to fall several times, my precautions against falling have caused more laughs than all the tumbles the others have taken. They are unkind enough to say that it would be impossible for me to fall down because I do not stand up in the first place. They are exaggerating, as they usually do when they talk about me. Why, the first day the ice was on, every lamp in the house was dry. Wasn't it heroic how I took one lamp across the icy yard to fill with kerosene from the barrel! Maybe it wasn't just courage that made me decide we could get along for one evening with a single lamp. But I didn't hear anyone offer to do the task for me.

It was my trip upstairs that my unfeeling family thought so funny. I am glad no teams or cars were passing along the road at that time. Our house is not yet completed. (In fact we moved in as soon as we started building, or so the neighbors say. It wasn't quite that bad—we had half the roof on and part of the floors down. Neighbors have to be entertained though, and they were most interested when a rain came before we had the roof quite finished.) We have no stairway yet. To get upstairs one must go out the back door at the south and around the house to the east where the front door may be reached by climbing a flight of stairs. There will not be so many steps when we get the yard graded and terraced so we can build the front porch.

To be safe I crept up the icy steps. At the top I was afraid to stand up. I couldn't get the door open without standing up to unfasten it. Finally I gave up and crept back down the stairs. Back on solid, although somewhat slickish, ground I discovered that my morale had deserted me. Like the first and only time I tried to skate I found that I couldn't stand on my feet just because I was afraid to stand on my feet.

I didn't call for help. No one could have heard me. If they had, I doubt that I would have received much help, only a heap of advice that would hinder my progress. With commendable bravery I managed to get back around the house and down the slick slope to the back door. The ice was a bit cold on my bare hands, but I prefer cold hands to a broken head.

After all, it wouldn't have mattered much if some of the neighbors had been going past to see me. For they heard all about it afterward. Families are so thoughtful about such matters.

WE are learning that a farmer who builds a house during his spare time is likely to take a long time at the task even if he has a talented wife, such as I, who also drives nails during her spare time. Having lived on farms virtually all our lives, I do not know how we happened to imagine that farm people have spare time. It is taking some months to finish our house, even though we employ every rainy or blizzardy day, many days that ought to be spent at other work, and every evening when we can get the chores done in time.

We have talked and talked of putting a bolt on the back door until we can finish putting on the lock. However, there are too many things to be done immediately, so we content ourselves by latching the screen door on the back porch and putting a chair against the inside door. Sometimes the wind gets too strong for the chair and we drive a nail into the temporary cottonwood casing to hold the door shut.

When we went to Grandma's Saturday night we forgot about the nail. We fastened the porch screen, put the chair against the door, and went out the front door, which we locked. It was the first time the six of us had spent the night away from home, so it had been a busy time getting ready to go. When we arrived home the next afternoon, we found the back door open and a layer of beautiful snow covering much of the kitchen and dining room floors.

We are spending next Saturday polishing the floor.

There are times when I'm not very enthusiastic about living in a house while it is being built. I grumble a bit about sawdust-flavored meals and dirt that tumbles down on the baby's face while he is asleep. It wouldn't be so bad if the building were going ahead all the time so the end of the pounding and sawing would not seem so far away. But the carpenter is also a farmer and dairyman, so his days at house-building begin late and end early. Sometimes he has to stop and fix the fires or get a bucket of water or take care of the babies a while so his wife can finish her writing.

Just because everybody has more to do than can be done there has been an epidemic of breaks among the farm machinery. Many of the implements are old because farm incomes have not been large enough to permit the purchase of many new machines in recent years. And the harvest has not been easy on them this year. The matted, tangled undergrowth in the meadows has broken mower parts and snapped off rake teeth. The small grain was down. Much of it had to be mowed, and that was not an easy task for a veteran mower. Ancient binders, too, had the most difficult labor they have had for a long time. Under the strain the rotted wood or cracked metal gave way, and repairs had to be made time after time.

Our steel drill has been in use nearly every day this summer. A drill and a scrap iron pile save a good many dollars that would have to be spent if new parts were bought each time something is broken. With the help of a thread cutter or die all minor repairing can be done at home with no expense and in no more time than a trip to town after repairs would require.

IT is true that 1934 can go down in history as the hottest summer and the dustiest period within the memories of the present generation, if not for all time. I have no desire to exist through another season so torrid. I didn't enjoy it even when I realized that if I lived through it I'd have something to tell the young people about when I grow old.

However, last year cannot take all the laurels for breaking records. I think 1935 has come out ahead of any previous year in the production of flies. If the fly population was ever any larger or the individual creatures any more ferocious than at present, it must have been a great many years ago. So far as I am concerned it will be all right if the present record is not exceeded or even equaled within my lifetime. That goes for snakes and mosquitoes as well. No wonder the weeds are taking the farms. The farm people are too busy slapping skeeters, shooing flies, and killing snakes to get anything else done!

If 1936 is going to follow the lead of its predecessors and eclipse all the other years in some way, I hope it isn't by giving us the coldest winter or the most politicians. We might have the fullest granaries, the biggest paychecks, or the best fishing for a change.

Many of the readers, in their letters, ask how we like our home after living in it a while. Those who have built their own dwellings are interested because they, too, spent days and nights planning and discarding plans before they decided how to build. Then changes were made as the building was being erected and at last they liked some of the things and did not like others.

We do like our house. The things we do not like are mostly the changes we made during the building process. Before we began building we spent months on the plans. There was a special reason for putting each thing where it was. When we made a change we were sorry for it nearly every time.

We had planned to have a cave opening from one of the back basement rooms. But we had to have the cistern at one corner and the sewer tile at the west side, so we gave it up. We believe now that it would have been all right to have made a small one under the front porch, but at that time we did not think it would do to put it in the front of the house.

We wish we had insisted on a steep, straight stairway closed off by a door rather than two steps in the dining room and a turn to the main stairway. The fireplace and range heat the dining room and kitchen nicely, but it would be much better if we didn't have to heat the stairway, too.

We wish we had built the kitchen chimney where we first planned it so one of the bedrooms would have been larger. We are not sorry we made the dining room shorter so the kitchen would have more room. It is better to be somewhat crowded on the days we open the dining room table full length than to be crowded in the kitchen every day.

L I V I N G four or five miles from town has its disadvantages. Before we left our home in a community that bordered town, we knew we'd miss having the post office, stores, and railway station so handy. But we had no idea that an isolated neighborhood had as many points in its favor as against it.

In previous years our neighbors came to help us if we were ill. In the pre–chinch bug era we exchanged work at threshing time. After the threshing was over we seldom saw each other unless we happened to be in town on the same day. Even those who attended the same church in town only caught glimpses of each other across the room. In the daytime we hurried home from church to get the noon meal. At night we were eager to get the kids back to bed before they became too tired. When we needed extra help we hired a man from town.

It is not that way here. It is too far to go to town to get hired help, so the neighbors help each other with their work. When we find the salt box, the baking powder can, or the flour bin empty, we do not hurry to town to get more—it is too far to go even when the weather is good. It is impossible to go even once a week when the roads are blocked with snow, so the mail carrier, the cream trucker, and all the other callers (except the stork, who makes his rounds as usual) are kept away from the rural districts. When a farmer goes to town he buys enough groceries and other supplies to last for two or three weeks. All the residents of the community send by him for the things they need. And when no one is going to town—we borrow.

The first day we lived here I was quite shamed when I couldn't find where I had packed the salt and had to send the boys to borrow some. Now I ask anyone to loan me what I need without a qualm because since that first day I have lent salt, rubber jar rings, yeast, soap, flour, and other household necessities from time to time. I have borrowed salt four times in less than three months. The last time the boss went to town he bought a twenty-five pound sack of it. Maybe I will not be borrowing salt again soon.

I like borrowing though. If it were not for borrowing, exchanging help, and sending to town by the neighbors, we wouldn't have much company. The people here, like those who live near town, think they are too busy to go visiting unless they have a legitimate excuse. And if we do feel the urge to go somewhere without an excuse we don't take Saturday afternoon off and go to town. We haven't acquired that habit of farmers near town. We wait until Sunday afternoon and go to see one of the neighbors—and gossip about all the rest of them. It's much more fun than going to town.

Living in the backwoods is pretty nice in some ways. I think I am going to like it. At least it isn't a lonely life. Oh my no, not half so lonely as living close to town.

5

Chinch Bugs, Boys, Pets, Neighbors

Most of the columns in this chapter originally appeared in the *Des Moines Tribune* during the years 1935 through 1938. The hot, dry summer of 1936 broke some of the heat records of 1934, and the farmers of southern Iowa were still plagued by chinch bugs, but the effects of the economic depression were starting to lessen. Most of the columns I have selected deal with life on the farm, our family, and the close neighbors.

A FARMER'S WIFE writes about an amusing experience she had in the autumn of 1934. She was visiting in a small Iowa city noted for its cool lawns and broad shady streets. "I suppose I didn't look so handsome. I'd survived that most terrible hot summer with drought and grasshoppers. Everyone in our vicinity looked and felt tired out.

"I was introduced to a very pretty girl by a mutual acquaintance. The girl looked startled and gasped, 'I never thought you'd look like that.' I thought it was funny but the speaker and the one who introduced us were very much embarrassed."

The summer of 1934 didn't improve the appearance of most of the farm residents around here either. And we didn't get rested up much of the next year with our task of building a new home while we were living in it.

Also, the youngest, who was born in August 1934 did a grand job of crying lustily until September 1935, which kept the whole family—who had to sleep in the dining room because the bedrooms were not finished—from sleeping more than an hour or two at a time. (Later we learned that the reason Irvin cried so much was that he had severe mastoid trouble, which was repaired by an operation when he was six.)

We visited our town one afternoon that fall during its usual exhibit of farm products. We hadn't been there since moving back to the home neighborhood after an absence of seven years; it had been nearly eight years since I had seen very many of the people I knew.

But I didn't do much visiting with old friends after all. Whenever I spoke to anyone I had to tell them who I was; I tired of that and quit speaking to anyone. At last, however, I spied a group that I had seen at infrequent intervals through the years and that I knew would know me. In their midst was a woman I hadn't seen since I was eighteen, twenty years before. She didn't know me, either.

"What's the matter? Didn't you think I'd get old like all the rest of you?" I asked.

"Well, I supposed you would look older—but not so much older," she replied soberly, to the huge delight of myself and the listening group.

Before then I had thought my afternoon was spoiled because nobody knew me. After that I found a shady bench and sat holding my fussing youngster and chuckling the rest of the afternoon. Whenever somebody passed without recognizing me I grinned at the thought that they, too, had no idea that I looked so much older.

VAUGHN and Charles had gone to bed, but they had to get up when they heard that Raymond's picture was in the paper. This household has heard much about Raymond during the last five years.

When the big boy of our family became old enough to go to school, Raymond was his chief subject of conversation. Seven-year-old Raymond was admired and respected for all the wisdom and superior strength his two years of seniority gave him. It was Raymond who sniffed at the idea of the primer folks washing before they ate their noon lunch. He had gone to school for two years and was over many of the sissy notions that mothers teach boys when they are little and have to stay home. He boasted that he was full of worms if boys got them by not washing before eating their school lunches.

I haven't heard so much about Raymond this winter. I haven't written anything about him in the column for a long time because his school is not our school any more. But he is no less their hero even though the lads of this family have not seen him for months. They are loyal. Their admiration has not been transferred to any of the big boys in the new school.

The picture of Raymond and his brothers with their fiddles brought forth many excited comments. Raymond, Lowell, Quincy, and Marmion were pointed out to me, although I knew them quite as well as my informants. Their names were in the paper anyhow; I could have read them. There wasn't time to answer half the questions that were fired at me in rapid succession. I guess answers weren't expected anyhow.

Why weren't Raymond's little brothers in the picture? Did I suppose they had to stay home and help their dad with the chores? Why did I suppose Raymond's mother went to Des Moines to the Farm Bureau meeting with the boys? Why was she in the picture? She didn't have a violin, did she?

After the boys had gone back to bed, I pondered over the last question. I wondered if the cameraman who took the picture of the Adams Brothers String Quartet for the *Tribune* realized how fitting it was that the mother was in the picture with the young musicians?

He couldn't know how many chickens she has raised and dressed for city folks to eat. He couldn't imagine how many dressed chickens it would take to pay for all the violin lessons needed to make a quartet good enough to play over the radio and at the conventions and other places they played. He could not know how much work it is to raise chickens. He couldn't know about the time a weasel killed a whole brooder house full of chickens that were to pay for next year's lessons and how more eggs had to be set to hatch a new brood. He couldn't know how hard it is for a mother with two babies and four schoolboys to grow a big garden, do enough canning for a family of eight, and yet find enough time to raise chickens and dress chickens and deliver them when she took the boys to the county seat for their music lessons.

He couldn't realize that she had dozens of milk bottles to wash and sometimes had to deliver the milk before she could get ready to take the boys to their lessons. He might think because the two babies are big boys now, big enough to go to school, that she would have less to do. Maybe she does or maybe her tasks are a bit different now, but when big boys have to spend much time practicing and when they have to play at entertainments before the evening chores are done there is plenty left at home to keep dads and mothers and small brothers quite busy.

Maybe the picture man guessed some of these things and the many others that are a part of the life of the mother of six boys who determines that each of the six shall have just as good a chance in this world as if he were an only child. Maybe he realized a little bit of this. Maybe that was why he included her picture in the paper with the boys, for that is where she belonged. She is just as much a part of the Adams Brothers String Quartet as any of her four eldest sons.

THE farm woman is in the kitchen cooking supper. Charles, her eight-year-old son is standing at the table poring over last year's almanac by the light of the kerosene lamp.

"Mother, when was the coldest winter, Mother?"

"I don't know."

"It was in 1709. The ground was frozen for three yards deep and the Medit ... Mediternean and Aderotic Seas were frozen over."

"Mother, when was the year without a summer, Mother?"

"Here, don't do that. You'll hurt the baby. Mother, make him come in here and help me take care of these kids," implores a voice from the dining room.

"Aw, can't I ever have a little time to read? I never get to read anything. Mother, don't you think ninety-three below zero would be pretty cold, Mother?" "Mother, would that freeze the thermometer, Mother? Would it break if it did freeze?"

"In the summer of 1816 there wasn't any summer, Mother. Mother, there was frost and snow every month of the year in 1816, Mother, as far south as Virginia, Mother."

"He will just have to come and help me. I can't manage. Here! Here! You will upset the lamp. I said to come in here right now," comes a shout from the dining room.

"Aw, I never will get to read this almanac. Mother, do you think eight below zero is very cold, Mother? That is the coldest it ever was in England. That was in 1913–14 and the river Thames froze over."

"Mother, aren't you going to make him come and help me before Bruce breaks something or hurts the baby?"

"Mother, what is the hottest country in the world, Mother? It was 134.1 degrees in Death Valley in 1913. It was up to 136.4 at some other place I can't pronounce one time though, Mother."

"Say, Charles, you don't need to think you can stay in there and read all the time. You don't need to think I'm going to do all the work around here all the time. I don't even get to see the funnies. Come and hold the baby, so I can look at Popeye."

"In a minute, Vaughn. Mother, how big is the biggest diamond? Mother, how many square miles are there in the area of the earth, Mother? Mother, what is the largest continent, Mother?"

"Come on now and stop that prattle. I want to see the funnies."

"All right. Mother, what are the names of the two largest islands, Mother?"

"Oh, Australia and—and England."

"Nope, Australia and Greenland. You don't know very much about geography, do you, Mother?"

"Mother, the deepest place in the ocean is 44,000 feet deep, Mother. Don't you think that is deep, Mother?"

"Mother, do you suppose the average population here would be 814 people to the square mile?"

"No, I don't think so."

"Well, it tells about a place here where there are that many people in India."

"Mother, what language do we speak, Mother? Is it the English language, Mother? There are more people who speak English than any other language. Mother, the teacher says . . .''

"Mother, Charles has just got to come in here and hold this baby."

"Aw, shucks, I never get to read the almanac or anything."

SATURDAY NIGHT at the county seat. Not just any ordinary Saturday evening, but the one particular one that comes just once each year. The Saturday night before school begins.

Boys and girls are choosing pencils, tablets, ink, pens, and new dinner pails. Everywhere the women are buying shirts and trousers, dresses, shoes, and hose for their broods. Everywhere tired daddies, who have spent the day hard at work on the farm, are taking care of the babies while the mothers shop. Half the babies are crying because they are not accustomed to being up so late. Small toddlers are getting cranky. So are some of the overworked clerks. And so are some of the would-be customers, who have to wait so long so make their purchases.

We can't blame the babies or their older brothers and sisters. They are too tired and sleepy to be reasonable. We can't blame the clerks. It is very trying to come to a customer who has been waiting half an hour and have her ask for a pair of overalls when she has no idea what size her boy wears, what price she wants to pay, or what color to choose.

We can't blame the mother. She has been so busy hurrying through the milking and supper work and getting all the youngsters ready for town that she hasn't had time to think of all that is needed, much less any particulars about a garment. She could have thought of some of it while she was waiting her turn. But she was thinking about how her feet hurt and how late it was getting and wondering if she had forgotten anything and if the baby was crying.

The shoe salesmen are just as busy as the clerks in the clothing stores. Their task is even more difficult. Lads who have gone barefoot all summer are inclined to think all shoes are too small for them. Little girls and their mothers often do not have the same opinions about what the well-shod schoolgirl should wear.

Perhaps the most bewildered of all are the mothers who are getting ready to send their first child to high school. It is a problem to choose clothing that will look well after going back and forth to school every day through all kinds of weather, especially for students who will make the trip on horseback each day. Too often the child and the parents cannot agree. Perhaps one is right, perhaps the other, or maybe both are a little bit wrong.

All in all, the last Saturday in August is not pleasant for parents or their progeny. It is easy to resolve that the shopping will be done earlier next year. But next year money will be just as scarce, farmers just as busy, and humans just as prone to prolong everything as long as they can. No doubt 1936 will see another frenzied evening much like August 31, 1935.

THIS morning I lighted the stove and put water on to heat for our cereal. The baby awoke and demanded his bottle. I put the cereal on to cook. I found clean shirts and stockings for the boys. Irvin fussed. I talked to him. Cut the meat and put it on to cook. Got out the biscuit pan and breadboard. Found Bruce's shirt for him where he had left it—on the baby's bed.

Took up the meat, which had begun to burn. Made gravy and mixed the biscuits. Tied a shoestring. Found a lost stocking. Cut out the biscuits. Quieted baby. Put biscuits in the oven. Packed school lunches. Baby fussed. Talked to him. Finally induced family to come to breakfast table.

One boy remembered he hadn't washed. Quieted baby. Ate breakfast. Hunted coats and mittens. Examined faces to see if they were clean enough to go to school.

But every morning is not like this one. Yesterday morning the baby cried all the while breakfast was being prepared. Bruce had an earache and had to be doctored and then had to have help in dressing. Other mornings there are other diversions.

But I am not deluding myself into thinking that I have more to do than anyone else. Lots of mothers are as busy during the three hours before time to go to school. Many people with no children at all are just as busy. Thoughts of how busy we are make us tired. Worry is worse than work, and self-pity is worse than either work or worry.

I like taking care of the baby and helping small boys get ready for school. So do the other mothers. So why complain or worry about it if it does take a little longer to get breakfast? Or fuss because the house is untidy? There isn't any need to feel sorry for ourselves. Let's save our pity for the mothers who were so tired and busy a few years ago and who no longer have any children at home to bother them.

ALTHOUGH it has been dry for so long that we have almost given up hope of getting any fall rains, the boss is hurrying with the soybean stacking lest we do get some downpours like those falling in other parts of the country. I guess he is tired tonight. I may not be exactly tired, but I'm glad tomorrow will be a day of washing, ironing, and tomato canning instead of another chicken-canning day.

I'm sure Effie May is tired. She slipped out of the barn where she was penned to keep her from getting through the gates as the loads of beans were brought up to the sheep pasture to be stacked. She has been out in the big pasture all day. It is pretty hard for Vaughn to find Effie May's mother when he goes after her at milking time, so it must have been quite a task for the ambitious calf. But she found her and milked her dry.

This night she didn't bother our neighbor when he came after his cows. This neighbor sold fourteen calves last week, and the mother cows have been giving voice to their grief in no uncertain manner.

One night earlier this week he came after the cows just about dark—he has soybeans to keep him in the field until late at night, too—and there was much bawling among the herd as he rounded them up to drive them out into the road, across the railroad track, and home. Effie May heard them. We were late, too, and she hadn't had any supper. She began to answer them. They came running back one at a time and lined up along our garden fence, each one sure it was her baby who was making such a fuss. Again their owner collected them and drove them the quarter mile back to the gate. I'm sure his opinion of Effie May agrees with ours.

But I started to tell you about today. Not to be outdone by a mere calf, the pigs nosed their way under the garden fence this afternoon and we found six of them admiring our beans and tomatoes. And tonight the plunger in the hog-well pump broke while water was being pumped to put the oats to soak. We had been so busy watching the clouds ever since the beans were mowed that we had forgotten there are a good many other things that can, and always do, happen during hay harvest besides rain.

Today's papers are tempting but, as much as I'd like to read them, it seems best to go to bed. Nothing has been said about it, but I shouldn't be surprised if I'd get to help repair that pump before the washing is started in the morning. I'd better get plenty of rest, so I will be in a good humor for wash-day. For if there is anything I hate more than helping haul a pump out of a well and putting it back again, I'm too sleepy to think of it right now. So, goodnight.

T HE telephone is a nuisance most of the time. It always rings at inopportune moments—when the baby is asleep, mealtime, or when the jelly is just ready to boil over. The line you want is busy or the people you are trying to call have gone to town or are out doing the chores.

From the far side of the garden you rush madly to the house to answer a persistent ringing. You choke down your wrath and politely inform the owner of the strange voice that you are not Alice or Nell or Mary but that the operator has given her the wrong number. You go back to the garden, and the ringing begins again.

"Let them ring. I told them once this was the wrong number," you growl. But soon you go back. "Hello," you yell crossly at a friend who is really calling you.

The telephone bill is always due at a time when the family pocketbook is empty. The batteries run down unexpectedly and then you get an important long distance call and can't make yourself heard.

But sometimes we are mighty glad to have a telephone to bother us. Two of the boys are quite sick. We may need to call the doctor. It is a comfort to know we can get him in a hurry if he is needed.

This morning I made four calls to find where one of our cows had gone. A call to a neighbor brought information about some of the fieldwork with which our menfolks are helping. Another call saved a trip to the home of a neighbor who wasn't there. We couldn't get the seed he sold us unless he was there to help measure it. A call from across the fields to let us know the missing cow was safe and that we needn't come after her if we were busy. And are we busy? This is April. A man phoned to see if we could get the seed he had sold us, and that was just what we were wanting to do. An acquaintance called with news from members of the family who live far enough away that we seldom get to see them but yet so close that we do not write letters often. The neighbor who borrowed one of our teams phoned at noon to find out how much grain the horses were used to having. One of the hogs has been off feed, and we may have to phone for the veterinarian.

Yes, the telephone is a nuisance—and a help. And, although I had to stop to answer a call meant for someone else before I was through writing this, I'm glad we have one after all.

WE were going to have company for the noon meal on Sunday. I wanted the dinner to be a little more attractive than the last time these guests had eaten at our house when we were not expecting them. That time we hadn't had much of anything but pie, potatoes, scalloped corn, chicken, and the fixings. There had been enough to eat, but when one knows visitors are coming it is nice to do some extra getting ready.

So this time the cook and I spent Saturday baking a burnt sugar cake, an ovenful of pumpkin pies, and dressing an enormous fat chicken and putting it on the porch to stay cool until we would be ready to pop the roaster in the oven. We made a tapioca fruit pudding, cooled it, and put it into twelve sherbet glasses. We cooked the cranberries just the way we like them and thought of more and more good things to cook every time we had finished what we were doing. For once everything went just right. That should have been a good enough hint. Nobody tracked in any mud, nor did anything we prepared to eat seem to fall short of perfection. To make sure that there would be plenty of light bread, we baked biscuits for breakfast and cornbread for dinner. Since we had plenty of pies, we cut one of them for supper to save preparing a special dessert for that meal.

Just as supper was ready the telephone rang. It was one of the expected guests. Of course, they were not coming. Guests never come when the house is clean and the meal is ready. Not to be daunted, I determined not to waste all that work. Surely someone would come home from Sunday school with us on the morrow and help us eat all that food. So sure was I that I didn't relent and put any of it on the supper table. Instead the family ate the pie, potatoes, beans, and other plain food previously intended for that meal.

Before bedtime two members of the family were complaining of feeling ill. By morning one of them was better, but two more joined the sick ranks and refused to eat breakfast. Three of us went to Sunday school, leaving the patients to keep fire in the stove to cook the chicken, the sweet potatoes, and Irish potatoes.

There were not very many at Sunday school. Only one of the women hadn't dressed a chicken and had it partly cooked and in the oven at home. And that one had promised to go home with her mother and help eat her chicken.

As we neared home, a car drove into our yard, but my hopes were dashed when I saw it was only a party of hunters who wanted to use the yard to eat the lunch they had brought with them. If I could have coaxed them within doors, I might have been able to get rid of some of the surplus food. But I made a very small dish of noodles and another small dish of dressing. Those of us who had appetites ate dinner and, later, supper.

And now it is Monday. Apparently there is plenty left for another dinner and a supper. My sons are not careful boys who can take pie, fruit pudding, or other perishables in their lunch. Nor do they care enough for chicken to want any of it. They can get rid of some of the cake, though. Until the weekly laundry and other first-of-the-week work is done, I don't believe there will be much bother about cooking at my house this week.

YES, I went to the *Register and Tribune* carriers' convention with my nephew Dallas and his chum. Dallas wasn't to blame. He didn't offer any objections, but it wasn't his idea. Boys planning to go on a trip and have a good time can't work up much enthusiasm about taking along an elderly aunt. It was his mother who made the suggestion, so there wasn't much Dallas could do about it without becoming impolite. Almost any boy can tell you how mothers are and what queer notions they get. However, Dallas wasn't quite so humiliated when he discovered that several of the other boys were burdened with mothers, big sisters, or other antiquated relatives.

A misunderstanding about the train schedule caused us to arrive at Albia nearly an hour and a half too early. How we regretted that lost half hour of sleep! Finally our train, bearing its noisy burden, pulled up at the station.

Once in our car we could no longer hear the commotion in the other coaches. No doubt the voices were as loud as before, but we couldn't hear them over the uproar in our own midst. At times in the past I've insinuated that it would be impossible for a dozen lads to make any more racket than the four at our house create. But I didn't know. After spending five hours in a coach with a pleasure-bent group, it seems quiet here with only four boys talking, shouting, and scampering through the house.

I blush to think that I have told my sons that other boys do not get so dirty as mine. Long before we reached Knoxville many of the shirts, slacks, and white shoes that had been spic-and-span as we waited at the Albia station were just as soiled as if my boys had been wearing them. When a boy is eight or ten or twelve he is too busy to be particular. A good many older boys were along, but they were not so much in evidence as the enterprising group that I have just mentioned.

Miraculously we arrived at our destination without having lost a boy out of a window. I went uptown, and my relieved escorts went with their colleagues to Riverview.

I hunted a shady spot to wait for the parade after finishing my errands. Many others likewise found the shade, so we were too warm and crowded for comfort. When Eleanor Roosevelt arrived necks were craned and there was much excited talk. The crowd hadn't known that she was to review the parade. She appeared to be merely a pleasant lady, not at all impressive as one might expect the president's wife to be and, like the majority of her sex, fond of talking.

Presently the parade began. One has to see 4,000 boys to get some idea of how many that is. I began getting stage fright when I thought of how many people read the state papers. If 100,000 of them read the farm page and if half or one-tenth of the farm page readers glance over this column sometimes—it scares me a little to think of it.

One onlooker in front of me, who was from the east and felt his superiority over us savages from the "wild" west, kept making remarks that were clever from his own viewpoint. Once he volunteered that the boys in the parade had "farmer" written all over them. That showed what he knew about it. Probably he thought all Iowa residents were farmers. Very few of the marchers looked like farm boys. Any Iowan could pick out a few. Most of them were the type that we see in the average county seat town out here in this "uncivilized" section of the world. They were less tanned, much less timid, and more self-assured in a crowd than country boys.

There isn't much difference in the heart of a boy wherever he is. I imagine the eastern boys are much like the farm, town, and city boys we know, even if they are groomed differently. If they are different, I'm not at all sure that it means they are any better than Iowa boys.

After the parade I found the particular Monroe County boys I wanted to see at the circus and stayed with them the rest of the day. It was a weary, disheveled group of boys in the Albia coach on the way home. But they didn't rest. They were doing their best to make a day of it. I wonder if there were not tired, cross boys in a good many Iowa homes Tuesday morning?

A pessimistic cuckoo in our maple trees has croaked for rain, dismally and hopelessly, for two entire days. Probably his ancestors have told him of the lovely rains that came almost every day during the summers of 1907 (or was it 1908), 1915, and 1927, and he is just voicing his regret that he did not live in the good old days. Or he may be one of those who believe that he who suffers in silence continues to suffer and he who complains the longest and loudest gets results.

The rain crow isn't the only one who would like to see a few showers. But it doesn't do any good to sit around and complain about the heat and dust. Probably fuzzy caterpillars taste better after a rain. No doubt the product now available for hungry cuckoos is rather tough and tasteless, for the apple and walnut leaves upon which caterpillars feast are getting dry.

But we don't hear the caterpillars complaining about it. They busy themselves with affairs over which they have control and to the best of my knowledge have wasted no time knocking the weather. The silly bird ought to be glad he has any kind of worms to eat, even if he can't get the juicy kind he likes best. And if he spent more time hunting food and less time grouching, he might find plenty of tempting morsels within flying distance. Just think what a story he is going to be able to tell posterity when he hears complaints about skinny, insipid worms.

IS there anyone besides me who can't carry on an intelligent conversation over the telephone if the phone is in a dark room? I can't think of a thing to say because I imagine the person at the other end of the line can't hear my voice. No doubt everybody felt that way when they first acquired telephones. I've heard people tell about being afraid to scold the children after they had installed the magic voice carrier lest the neighbors might hear them. Evidently they had no fear their gentle tones wouldn't carry over the new contrivance!

As soon as this is printed some cruel member of my family will read it and remark that I can't carry on an intelligent conversation anywhere at any time. But then families are noted for their heartlessness.

Many a potential case of swelled head has been nipped in the bud by caustic remarks made by relatives of the owner of the enlarged head. All of us have kinfolks who do not appreciate us. It is one of the unavoidable cankers that has to be endured. It isn't much consolation to realize that we pester them as much as they harass us. We take them down a notch or two once in a while for their own good.

Flattery is a good thing if we don't get too much of it. A little criticism mixed with it helps all of us. If no one ever applauded when we did well or complained when we made mistakes we would become a mediocre race.

The hardest thing is to do what we think is right when others think we are doing wrong. Everybody can't see all matters alike. We have to develop our powers of reasoning on our own and refuse to depend upon the opinions of others. They might be mistaken part of the time. It is well to listen to them, though, for sometimes we, ourselves, might be in error.

All of which is a long way from talking over a telephone in a dark room. It just goes to show how one's thoughts can ramble.

THE candidates have begun traveling the country roads again. We haven't seen any of them since the first of June. How we missed them! There had been so many of them—all so interested in the farmer's troubles and problems that we hardly knew how to get along without them.

As the days went by and none of them reappeared we wondered what had happened. Where were they? It did not seem possible that such a hardy species could have become extinct in so short a period. Yet not a single specimen was visible. We just didn't understand it. Probably they were merely hibernating through the hot summer months. At any rate they have appeared on the scene again—droves of them—as large as life and twice as friendly.

For a while it seemed as if the farmer's lot was to be a difficult one. Poor crops, dry wells, and no grass for the livestock. However, the political aspirants promise us relief from all our troubles. I'm not at all sure they aren't responsible for these beautiful rains that have filled up discouraged wells and brought the green back to the brown pastures.

We feel mighty good about it. For one reason, each of these well-dressed, prosperous-appearing visitors of ours has assured us that if he or she is elected we will not be forgotten—our welfare will be considered first of all when any questions arise. That would encourage anybody. In the past farmers have been considered as people for only a few weeks just before the primaries and again for a few more weeks just before the November elections. In years in which no elections were held, we were just plain rubes who didn't count.

The Republican candidates assure us it will be a stiff fight but the Republicans, if elected, will stop this wild spending, assure better prices for farm products by keeping out foreign competition, and do a hundred and one other things that will restore this great nation to normal.

The Democrats assure us it will be a stiff fight, but they, if elected, will continue their sound program that has lifted us out of the depression and do a hundred and one things to make times even better than at present.

My Republican neighbor says the Republicans will be elected because all the farmers and businessmen will vote for them in order to put a stop to all this graft.

My Democratic neighbor says the Democrats will be re-elected because all the farmers and men on relief will vote for them because of the good they have done in the last four years.

It looks as though the farmer is going to have a mighty easy time of it for the next four years, no matter who wins.

WOMEN like to laugh at the difficulties their menfolks encounter when they try to batch for a short period. However, most of the Joans find it just as hard to do Darby's work in his absence as it is for him to do feminine tasks.

Late yesterday afternoon the man of the family was called to the bedside of his father, who was quite ill. As soon as he left, the herd sire jumped over a high wire fence and hung himself on the wire. When he did get loose he had to be driven back to the pasture. After many delays the big boys mounted the work team and went after the cows while I started to do some of the other chores. But the work didn't progress very rapidly.

Any farm woman who has chored by herself knows just how many things can go wrong. Even the pet goat thought up some new things to do. He jumped upon the doghouse and from there to the roof of the implement shed. When he scampered over the shingles it was just too much for the two little boys. The baby began to scream with fright and his brother joined the chorus. That pleased Billy. He likes to be the center of interest. He jumped off the shed and hopped into the wagon where the boys were standing. A whack from my stick sent him back to the roof again before he had a chance to hit either of the little ones.

In despair I attempted to put the lads to bed before I did any more of the work. The baby wanted to be rocked. Bruce declared he wasn't sleepy. Just at dark Vaughn and Charles came with the cows. Neither small boy was asleep. Our lantern is useless without a wick and is therefore useless at the present time. I wasn't very enthusiastic about taking two sleepy, cranky babies to the dark barn with me. Besides I was a bit squeamish about tackling some of the flighty heifers the boss has been milking. So despite protests I shut the door behind me, leaving two tearful lads with the cook.

Long before the fifteen cows had been milked, the baby had cried himself to sleep as he stood with his head leant over the couch. Neither of the boys is a talented milker. Feeling around in the dark for milk stools, buckets, and the waiting cows isn't very fast work anyhow. Once I poured one cow's milk into a bucket that was brimming full already.

At last the milking and separating were over. I carried one five-gallon bucket of milk to the squealing porkers who had had neither corn nor soybeans as usual. I left the rest on the back porch to be carried off after daylight this morning. I blush to say that I decided to leave the cows with the young calves until morning to save getting them out of the lot and back in again when daylight came. I carried the sleeping youngsters to bed without bothering to wash their feet or undress them.

Dick came back this morning in time to milk four of the cows. If he has to go back to sit up again tonight, I'm planning to start the chores very, very early. I may be okay as a helper, but I don't think I'd make a very good farmer by myself.

THE unbelievable has happened. Whenever a home or the clothing of anybody in it catches on fire, the water bucket is empty. Such things just don't happen when there is water in the house. But right here in this neighborhood, in the house down at the foot of the hill, there was an exception to this rule.

Iona, who lives down there with her two brothers, thought she smelled smoke. Like all brothers, whose privilege and duty it is to make fun of everything their sisters say, Francis and Lloyd scoffed at her. Even as you and I, when our brothers laugh at us, she went upstairs grimly determined to find a fire or die in the attempt to prove they were wrong. Triumphantly, albeit a bit frightened, she shrieked at what she saw. They believed her that time. Lloyd grabbed the telephone crank, rang six shorts so that everybody would come to the phone, and gave the alarm.

I heard him, climbed our stairs in nothing flat, and ran out on the front porch screaming for Dick. Over on the next hill Leta heard him and scurried out the back door, yelling for Howard and Gene. Away down in the timber the boss heard my screeches. Back in their far pasture Gene and Howard heard Leta's yells. There may not be any female Samsons in this neighborhood, but our lungs are marvelously strong. Our menfolk are well trained, too. In less time than it takes to tell Dick and Vaughn appeared out of the woods and ran down the hill toward the fire. Charles did the quickest job of getting into his cap, coat, and rubbers that he had ever done. He headed lickety-split down the hill. Over the hill by the schoolhouse I saw a grey team coming at a swift trot. Leta's menfolk were on their way, too.

Meanwhile, at the scene of the fire Francis grabbed the water pail, dashed up the stairs, and threw the contents in the general direction of the blazing roof. As Iona happened to be in the way the water went on her instead of the fire. One of the boys climbed out through the hole the fire had burned in the roof, and from there he put out the fire with three more pails of water his brother brought to him. I'm a bit hazy on this point, but I can't believe there were three more pails of water in the kitchen. I've been there, and their water bucket and teakettle are perpetually empty just as are those in many another farm kitchen. By the time the boss and the boys had run the half mile down our hill and the greys had trotted briskly down the other half-mile slope, the fire was out.

No doubt the boys had as difficult a task repairing the roof as Iona had in cleaning the water and charcoal from the floor. Yet at that I'm mighty sorry for her. You see, I am a sister, too. And a few times, a very few times, it has been conceded that I was right. When that happened I was very, very sorry I hadn't been wrong. And I was very, very glad when I was wrong so that my brothers would forget about the time I had been right. I'll bet Iona will be happy the next time she loses an argument, so they can forget how presumptuous she was in finding a fire that they had declared did not exist.

THEY are telling a good one on Homer. Those of us who hear it repeat it with glee, for he who has teased us unmercifully whenever we made mistakes has been caught in one himself. He never spares our feelings one bit no matter how we squirm or protest that he makes things out worse than they really are. So far be it from any of us to spare him.

Mary and Homer were in a car wreck. I don't know just how it happened but Homer tried to go around a corner too fast or something. He cut the corner too short, got off the pavement into the gravel, and things happened. Homer received a couple of broken ribs and some bruises, his son and nephew both lost the seats of their trousers, and Mary was rather seriously hurt.

She stayed at her daughter's home in town for some time while receiving medical treatment. When she began to talk about returning home her husband decided it was time for him to clean house. He didn't want Mary to know how it had looked while he and the boys were batching. I don't know just what agonies Homer underwent during the housecleaning process. Doubtless he learned it wasn't as easy as milking cows, pitching hay, or cultivating corn.

Finally he phoned his daughter and asked if it would hurt anything to get the linoleum wet. He didn't want to spoil it, but he couldn't make it shine like it did when the better half was doing the housekeeping. It seemed as though there were streaks of dust or mud or something that just wouldn't sweep off. He was thinking of taking a damp cloth and wiping some of it off, but he didn't know whether such a proceeding would be safe.

Since the telephone call was made on a party line, somebody heard it because all of the neighbors listened for Homer's ring to see how Mary was coming along. So even though the rookie housekeeper didn't tell any of his other troubles at his new task, it is going to be a long time before he hears the last of the linoleum episode. At least I hope so. It took Homer a long time to forget some of the things I hoped he'd forget to mention every time he saw me.

MA R C H is here with its usual offering of snow, sleet, and rain; warm days and cold ones; mud and frozen earth; blustery days and mild pleasant ones. When the sun shines and the mercury goes up into the fifties I sit here at the desk wishing I didn't have to write so I could clean house, get ready to make garden, and hunt a place to keep some baby chicks. I listen to the cackling, singing, and crowing of the poultry and the happy noises of the children playing in the yard.

At present the youngest isn't getting much enjoyment out of the warm air and sunshine, though. He is out on the front porch crying as lustily as only a very tired and sleepy youngster can weep. He wants the front screen to stay open. No matter how hard he pushes it open the strong spring brings it back. Once he came in the house to have me tie up his thumb, deeply gashed, where the stubborn door crashed shut against it. With a rag around the bleeding member he went back to his futile task. Like some of the rest of us, he has found out that getting angry doesn't help matters but he isn't going to admit it. It doesn't do any good to lose our tempers when things we hate to see happen do come to pass, but we can't see that unless it is somebody else who is fighting the inevitable.

That truck driver who had troubles out here on the hill the other day ought to see the boy trying to make the door stay open. The trucker's steady flow of language had no more effect on the mud than the lad's screams have on the banging screen. No, no more results than your rebellion or mine when we were given new proof of our insignificance in this universe.

Irvin will soon forget his troubles if he is brought into the house and put to bed for his afternoon nap. And I'm going to go get him just as soon as I get this written. Maybe I'll bribe him to sleep by rocking him. I don't claim to be a modern mother in all respects even if I am a bit cranky about diets.

By far the greater part of the worries of all of us are forgotten after we get sleep and rest. A good many of them are as foolish and unnecessary as the task of pitting his small strength against a strong door spring that the two-year-old has imposed upon himself.

6

Artists, Rainy Days, Hospital Sojourns

This chapter covers a period of more than a year, during which Dick suffered an eye injury in February and underwent a cataract operation that summer. Before Christmas I, too, spent some time in the hospital. Farm editor Russell of the *Des Moines Tribune* put a note of explanation in the paper to account for my missing columns. I received letters from all over Iowa, most of them from the western two-thirds of the state. Since there were three hospitals in Ottumwa at that time, some of the letters went to each of the two wrong hospitals but eventually reached my bedside.

Luckily for me my family brought my typewriter on one of their visits. I managed to write a few columns during some of my better days.

From time to time various readers came to see us in our hillside dugout. The four-year-old who sent the colored pictures became acquainted with our sons, but as he grew up and attained the dignity of being a schoolboy with playmates near his own age he rather ignored me. An old woman of thirty years is not very interesting. However, our friendship has been renewed. To our mutual surprise he was one of my instructors at an Elderhostel at the University of Iowa in 1980. It is a bit difficult for me to treat him with the respect due a university professor with a doctor's degree. I think of him as the little boy who told his mother I was as bad as she was when I worried that he, with my two sons and other readers' sons who had reached the mature ages of six, seven, and eight, were in danger because they were too near the edge of the diving board at Lake Ahquabi. He assured her they were *that* far—measuring off a distance of some three or four inches—from the end of the board. The snapshot taken by one of the group proved he was right.

NUMEROUS pencil marks and crayon drawings adorn our walls. They are the most numerous here in the dining room, where the fireplace tempts the whole family to collect in winter. The plywood walls appeal to the amateur artist or the lad who feels that he needs to practice with the pencil so he will know how to write when he gets big enough to go to school.

If painting or varnishing had been done, it wouldn't be very difficult to clean off the scribblings and cartoons drawn by our gifted four-year-old and his younger brother. However, paint and varnish cost money. So do many other things. Like so many other people we buy what seems to us the most essential things when there is money, and when there isn't anything in the family purse we stop buying. To date we have stopped each time before interior paint and varnish arrived at the top of the list of articles wanted.

At first I washed soiled spots, writing, and works of art from the walls but that darkened the wood. The decision was made that it would be best to use sandpaper to remove the dirt and the artistry just before we were ready to apply the varnish. It has been difficult to stifle the feminine instinct to scrub and clean, but on the whole I have done quite well. Other duties permit me to forget the masterpieces produced by stubby pencils and broken crayons until visitors arrive. Then every mark and fingerprint glares at me as I sit and try to make myself believe the guests haven't noticed many of the things I don't want them to see. In desperation I resolve to do many things that I forget about until the next time there are callers to entertain.

The plastered walls upstairs have fared better. There are fingerprints and marks, but not quite so many. There is more room up there to run and play, more toys, and dozens of things to examine that the small busybodies wouldn't be allowed to have if any of the rest of us knew what they were doing. The marks are pretty bad under the west window in the big boy's bedroom. He didn't like it at all when he saw what had been done. But the bed has to be somewhere, so I put it where it would hide those long black marks. It is all right so long as I don't forget and move the bed to another corner.

I've been thinking that if boys didn't grow up so rapidly that they are ready to go to school and acquire dignity almost before we know it—if that period from ten months to five years were any longer—it would be well to make our walls of slate.

In one room we see no results of the lads' attempt at interior decorating. The felt base floor covering that we used for the bathroom walls hasn't appealed to them like the nice clean wood and plaster of the other rooms. We used it there for we thought it wouldn't matter if water were splashed about during the ablutions of our four heirs or if someone forgot and ran the supply tank over when they were pumping water. Luckily for us, it is a poor place to draw pictures—I might say it is pencilproof as well as splashproof.

T H E R E is a fire in the fireplace today. The house was warm enough without it, but the heat from the blaze is proving very useful to dry the many pairs of overalls, shirts, and other masculine apparel that has been worn during the showers we have been receiving.

Vaughn and Dick each have three pairs of muddy overalls and all their everyday shirts, caps, and coats—with the exception of those they are wearing right now—strewn about on the chairs, fireplace screen, and every available location. The two youngest have almost as many garments to be dried, even though it does not seem necessary for them to have gone down to the lower pasture yesterday when a big rain was coming up. Nor for them to have helped (?) when their father and two big brothers were driving the spring pigs to different quarters this morning. Even Charles, who doesn't mind being my assistant as long as no one teases him about doing girl's work, has two sets of bedraggled garments.

It was raining so hard that the men of the family left me to mix the bread, get breakfast, and help the two youngest get dressed while they were doing the morning milking. Other outside work was left until after the morning meal and shower were over. So I do not have so many things to dry for myself. Just now I hung up my hat and one of the two coats I wore while we were milking and tending to the cows last night. They are dry at last, in spite of the terrible soaking they received while we were trying to make indifferent mothers claim some hungry but timid and foolish little calves.

I'd like to scrape some of the mud off the back porch and dining room floors so I could mop before another rain comes. But another more essential duty confronts me. Five of these wet shirts and five pairs of the blue denims must be dried before that dark cloud hanging over there reaches this part of Soap Creek. Then five gentlemen will be demanding something to wear. I might be able to find something for Bruce and Irvin. But the other three have nothing in their scanty wardrobes suitable for wearing in the muddy out-of-doors. The blanket-lined coats that were sopping last night are merely dampish at present. Presently I can put them away, I hope.

The cloud is drawing nearer. The sky is darkening. Doubtless there will be other dripping jackets and pantaloons to take the place of these that are partially dehydrated. In the meantime, since the other members of the family seem more concerned about finding excuses to stay outdoors in the downpours than they are in the ways and means of drying wet clothing, it is up to me to see if I can find any wood dry enough to burn.

Here comes the youngest. Soaked to the waist. I needn't be told he has been wading. He doesn't have to be in a torrential downpour. He can get the same result from a small, muddy water puddle. The mopping will have to wait.

THIS morning the youngest son came downstairs and ordered a birthday cake with whipped cream on it. One of the cousins had a birthday Saturday and there were two cakes in honor of the occasion. We agree with Irvin that it isn't quite fair if we can't have a birthday cake, even though there are no January birthdays in our family.

So we made the birthday cake. I did most of the work, and the two small boys offered the advice. Perhaps it was the superabundance of the advice, the attempts to help, or maybe the thoughts of other tasks awaiting me, but I became a bit mixed up. Probably I was thinking of making biscuits—which isn't strange considering that biscuits have to be made every morning and cake only two or three times a week—I put in two heaping spoons of baking powder. After handing the pan in which the batter had been mixed to my two assistants, I licked my fingers. The taste was rather bitter for cake batter. However the pan was scraped clean. The only objections were offered by Bruce, who insisted he didn't get nearly so much as his younger brother. In the oven our culinary creation had every appearance of being quite palatable. It raised nicely, cooked quickly, and smelled like birthday cake, as the lads informed me every time I opened the oven door. So I didn't worry much about having been unduly generous with

the leavening. My family does not insist on perfection in all
things. At mealtime quantity becomes more important than qual-
ity.

Luckily, the Christmas toys engaged the attention of their
young owners and they were busy upstairs with trucks, blocks,
and the once-velvet dogs at the time I took the pan out of the
oven. I put it and its contents on top of the oil stove in the
laundry room without being bothered by requests for samples. I
whipped the cream while I was getting our noon meal prepared.
I cut four squares of the cake and put the rest of it safely out of
sight. Each of us ate his dessert after the noon meal. We didn't
notice any baking powder taste. No sir, it tasted like birthday
cake. The rest of the cake was cut into six squares and a big
dishful of cream was whipped for the suppertime dessert. Again
every plate was scraped clean.

Just because there are only six of us and we don't have very
many birthdays is no reason why we can't have birthday cake
oftener than six times a year. It is a long time from my natal day
in February to the last of August when the birthdays of the men
of the family begin. We have voted for more and bigger birthday
cakes.

T H E man who is trying to sell us an electric lighting plant
says that warm weather and the busy season are approach-
ing. We believe him. He also says that summer is the time
of the year when a farmer needs electric lights more than any
other time for the work days are so long. He says the farmer gets
up at four o'clock, chores by lantern light, and works until late
at night before he comes in to do the evening chores.

I believe it would be a good idea if salesmen who deal with
farmers would make themselves acquainted with conditions. The
salesman ought to learn that a lantern or electric light is unnecessary at four A.M. in summer. It might be wise for him to figure out
how much sleep a farm family would get if the working hours
lasted so long that a light was needed for three or four hours
before bedtime and for a similar period each morning. If he
didn't want to get up early enough to see for himself just when
daybreak comes, he could learn by looking in an almanac. The
country people I know use their lanterns, or electric lights if they
have them, a great deal more in winter than in summer. Most of
them work as hard in winter as they do in summer.

The best time for a farmer to buy a lighting plant is when

he has the money to pay for one, regardless of how many hours it will be used during the summer months. Time passes too quickly to make one season better than another for making such a purchase. The days are either getting shorter or longer all the time. We need no agent to tell us that. All farm women want modern conveniences, and they are getting them as fast as they can afford to. They don't want salesmen to tell them what they need. They want to know which lighting plant, or which furnace, or which something else is the kind most suitable for their purpose.

A G A I N the plans of mere mortals have gone astray. After three weeks of working in the house, the boss announced that he would have to lay aside the saw, hammer, plane, square, and level and begin work in the timber. Quite an amount of sawdust, shavings, discarded ends of boards, and crooked nails can accumulate all over the house in three weeks, even though the assistant carpenter did what cleaning she could when she wasn't cooking, washing dishes, doing the laundry, or helping with the carpenter work.

So no objections were voiced. There will be another winter next year. There has been every year in the past. No doubt we can finish the house then. So it was a relief that I could revel in that feminine game of housecleaning that so delights all women.

Late Saturday afternoon the sawing and hammering ceased. We piled up the unused boards and swept the entire house. While the others were at the chores I mopped the kitchen, dining room, and bathroom and washed some of the windows. There wasn't much for supper, but things began to have more the appearance of a home and less that of a factory.

Nor was I the only one who did a bit of preparation for the next week's work. After supper the newly retired carpenter sharpened his ax and made inquiries about wool socks and high-cut shoes. (He knew where they were, but it's a habit like my weekly statement that I'll never get the washing done before noon this time. I do though, and he finds the clothing, towel, hammer, or whatever it is without help.) The chores were done swiftly Monday morning. The head farmer seized his ax and disappeared. With regret I had to give up all thoughts of housecleaning until the long neglected mending was completed. I had to put a patch on the elbow of a shirt sleeve before the boys could go to school.

Before noon the woodchopper was back at the house. A

thorn bush he had cut down had scratched the pupil of one eye. No more wood or sprouts have been cut. No housecleaning has been done. Some days the livestock are fed and watered. Other days some of them have no hay. Sometimes some of them have no water, which is much worse than neglecting the house or permitting brush to grow.

The doctor has said that there is a chance that the sight of the eye may not be completely gone. He may be able to see to some extent in spite of the scar that hinders vision. The patient is to stay in bed until the inflammation is reduced so the eye specialist can tell something about the eye's condition.

It isn't necessary for me to explain to farm people just how much time he is spending in bed. He doesn't have the strength to be outside long—perhaps an hour at a time, perhaps longer—then several hours on the couch and treatment of the injured eye and back again to help the boys with the tasks they cannot do alone. Yes, he is staying in bed—as does any farmer so long as he is able to wobble out to see about the stock.

O N E member of the family who objects strenuously when he discovers I have written something about him has had his feelings hurt again. Charles says it is bad enough for a boy to have to do housework without having his ability as a dishwasher advertised. I didn't know he objected to working in the house. He never complains about it. I've promised to be more careful in the future. Perhaps he won't mind if I inform you that he doesn't have to do any work at present that is beneath him. Since the boss has been handicapped by an injured eye, two small boys are kept pretty busy on Saturdays and before and after school. Choring and hauling wood have been big tasks for them because of the ice-covered ground.

Their dad helps as he can in spite of pain and weakness. The doctor who is to operate on him later has promised that the pain will lessen soon and that partial sight will be restored after his operation.

Nothing I write about the two youngest members of the family bothers them. It is quite different when the three eldest find their names in print. Now that Dick cannot read I might talk about him. But somehow—because he doesn't like to have his illnesses mentioned, because he likes to pretend that he doesn't do much work, because he knows that I know how he feels about some of the things I might say about him—I don't want to say those things even if he wouldn't know anything about it.

So I'll continue to write about two small boys, Nig the dog, Felix the cat, the chickens, and livestock. Then there will be no wounded feelings. But I will be thinking of other things even though I cannot write them. I'll be thinking of sleepless nights when the sufferer walked the floor, of his clumsy attempts to get his own hot-water bottle and hot packs because he didn't want to bother me. I can write of many things—the ice, the weather, livestock, chores, and the many things that are happening on this farm every day. If I make mistakes, if my words are not well chosen, and if my sentences are a bit unconnected, perhaps you will be lenient and remember that you, too, have been through times when your mind was not on your work.

Relatives and neighbors have done what they could, even though they too have had illness and an overabundance of chores. Even an insurance agent who stopped one cold day and found the head farmer too ill to talk to him insisted upon helping two small boys with chores.

There is much that is bad in the world, but much more that is good. When trouble comes it is good to know that the world has not forgotten us.

A day or two after Dick had hurt his eye Ottis Davis brought us a load of wood, his steel-wheeled tractor with the big lugs traveling over the icy hills with no difficulty. It was a very welcome surprise. Dick told Charles to keep one cow to milk, whichever one he liked best, and to turn the others dry as fast as he could. That isn't very easy to do when one is milking Jerseys, so he had to milk them once a day for quite a while. Vaughn had his hands full with the other chores, and I couldn't help them much. Because of the ice Vaughn could ride his sled down the half mile to the mailbox on the way to school and on the way home ride the half mile down the other hill from the school to the mailbox, thus saving time to spend on the chores.

The thorn had gone completely through Dick's eye. Six months later he was to have cataract surgery. His Uncle Frank Hoffman spent some time with us that summer and helped with the work.

The day before the operation there was a bad wind and hailstorm. The livestock came rushing in from the west pasture, and as the wind blew the gates open they ran across the road and into the east pasture. I had never seen stock so frightened. Rain and hail followed the wind. Our roof was ruined by the large hailstones, the north window in the library was broken, and the huge hailstones

blew across the library and living room and piled up along the
south living room wall. Our haystacks were blown down, one
through the fence and into Inez Williams's pasture. Dick's Uncle
Frank and the boys took care of the stock and rehung the gates and
doors. Boards were nailed over the broken window.

Early the next morning we had to go to Ottumwa for Dick's operation. I had intended to stay only the first night with Dick at the
hospital, but the surgeon thought that I should stay one more night
because Dick was still delirious. The phone lines were blown down
during the storm, so I couldn't phone to tell the family I was not
coming home when they expected me.

When I got back Dick's mother and his brother's wife were
there. They had cooked the noon meal for Uncle Frank, Dick's father and brother Rube, Lloyd Stocker, and Charley Blumer, who
had rebuilt our haystacks. Uncle Frank asked if I would be afraid
to stay alone. I told him I had done lots of things I was afraid to
do. So he stayed and helped the boys chore, and when Dick got
home from the hospital, Uncle Frank was still there to help care for
him.

Dick wasn't the only one to have to go to the hospital. A few
months later I had an operation. The next three columns relate to
it.

F R O M my hospital bed I can look out the window and see
a house. It has been painted grey—or possibly white—at
some time far back in the past. It's rather grimy now, but
the black trim on the door and window casings stubbornly refuses to surrender to the ravages of weather and coal smoke.

On this side a porch runs the full length of the building. At
first I thought it was a back porch. I saw a small boy with a toy
automobile emerge from one of the doors and other people coming out of other doorways until I was quite sure each of the four
doors was the entrance to the domicile of a different family. A few
moments ago, upon raising my head, I noticed that under this
porch is another porch onto which another four doors open. From
my second-story window this was not evident at first.

Then I noticed the chimneys, three of them on this side of
the house. Apparently the families who inhabit the two middle
apartments utilize the same chimney. And on the other side of
the house are three more chimneys just like them. To an amateur
sleuth like me that means that there is another double-decked
porch on the opposite side of the house with four doors and four

galvanized washtubs for each of the two floors of the porch. It means that sixteen families live in this soot-marred building, all living under that roof with its green covering flecked with traces of this afternoon's snow not yet discolored by the smoke and soot that is bellowing with such enthusiasm from the six chimneys.

So this must be the front and only porch for the four families, just as the porch below is the front and only porch for the families on the lower floor. And the double porch (if there is one) at the other side of the house is the only entrance for the inhabitants of that portion of the house.

For each door there are two windows. Through these windows I can see into the two middle rooms. In one a woman is drying dishes. In the other a round table covered with a clean white cloth and places set awaits a meal that is not quite ready or a member of the family who hasn't arrived.

It is getting dark. I cannot see the snow on the roof, but the chimneys are visible in the gathering dusk.

A man carrying a lunch box enters the door at the corner of the house. Earlier this afternoon I had seen a messenger boy on a shiny red bicycle park his wheel on the porch and go in at that door to remain for some time. To eat a meal, I had supposed. Later a somewhat smaller boy was seen going in and out the same door as if carrying out ashes and doing similar chores. The light is turned on as the man enters. I am beginning to suspect that there is no woman at this house to prepare a meal for this man and his two sons. Unprincipled snooper that I am, I wish I could see in at the window hidden by the wing of the hospital.

A family is gathered around the round table in the other apartment. Somebody is filling glasses from a pitcher and passing the water around.

The light is turned off in the apartment occupied by the workman, the messenger boy, and his younger brother. The other seven apartments are lighted. I'm sure nobody but a man could prepare a meal, eat, and wash the dishes so quickly. Or perhaps, and the thought comforts me, this family takes their meals away from home.

I'm going to watch this particular door with interest during my sojourn in this room. There is another family without a woman cook some twenty miles from here in whose welfare I am deeply interested. Maybe that is why I am so concerned about these three strangers who do not know that I exist.

SO many letters have come that I have had to give up my plan to answer each of them personally. This column will have to be the answer to all of you who wrote and sent cards, photos, or handkerchiefs. The nice things you said about what I write pleased me and made me feel humble at the same time. If I had known that scores of you were going to write I don't believe I would have been so homesick those first few lonesome days.

To those of you who want to know my address at home, it is Moravia, but if you forget you can write in care of the *Tribune*. Several former residents want to know in what part of Monroe County I was born; I was born in Urbana Township, one mile west of the Wapello County line and two and one-half miles north of the Appanoose County line, in the first house west of the Franklin schoolhouse in the same room in which my dad was born and died. At present I live two miles west and a half mile south, near the Urbana Center Church.

Yes, Knoxville reader, I know your father and see him often. He was a friend of my dad's in his lifetime.

To all of you who expressed disappointment that the "Farm Woman" doesn't write every day, I, too, wish that were possible. It is pleasant to know that you miss me the days you do not hear from me.

The three-year-old is helping me, so it is somewhat difficult to sort out the letters that have questions I want to answer.

I'll have to tell the one who wished I would soon be strong enough so this smallest child could sit on my lap again how he prepared for bed and went to sleep on my arm the first evening I was home.

And the boss, hardly able to be up at all, sat by the bed and told me of the first night I was gone. The youngest had gone to bed fully dressed. When it was suggested that his shoes be removed he issued the ultimatum that they were to stay on his feet until Mother got home so they wouldn't get lost. However, his garments were removed after he went to sleep and they didn't get lost, so he didn't object to undressing after that.

I can sit up some now and hope to be walking some in a few more days. "No work for a long time," say the doctors.

Tell the four-year-old who sent the pictures he colored that we enjoyed them very much, although I had so much assistance in opening the mail that morning that I didn't know in which envelope my two youngest sons found it.

And Myra, Millie, Iva, Blanche, Verla, Hazel, Maxine, Ruth, Mae, Florence, Luella, and all the others—there is so much I'd like to say to every one of you. But I do not have the strength to write many letters now. When I can sit up more Charles is going to help me locate your homes on the map. I didn't realize our home state had so many towns whose names I hadn't heard. And when I write articles for the *Tribune,* they'll be especially for you. It is much easier to write to real people than to those shadowy beings to whom my first columns were addressed some eight or nine years ago.

G R A D U A L L Y this vacation that began four weeks ago is becoming less vacationlike. It doesn't take long to forget how many garments can get torn and worn in a few weeks when no mending is done. Nor does it take long to forget how good work seems after a period of illness.

While my three dictators were at the morning chores, I did the sweeping. I was quite sure they wouldn't notice it had been done, so I wouldn't get scolded. I didn't sweep under the desk, sewing machine, cupboard, kitchen cabinet and bathtub, or behind the stove, yet it was as much fun as if every corner were shining clean. Cobwebs no longer leer at me. They know, and I know, that they cannot reign much longer. One of these days war will be waged on them and I have no intention of being the loser. The lint in the stairway and the toys strewn about in the upstairs rooms worry me not at all. Didn't I sweep the dining room, kitchen, and bathroom this morning?

I'm getting dinner all by myself. Of course, Charles brought the meat into the kitchen and helped me put it on to cook. And my mother peeled the potatoes and my sister-in-law made the noodles when they were here yesterday afternoon. But I'm the one who is having the fun of cooking them. I'm pretty sure I could dry dishes, too, if they would permit me, but they insist that I do not get them dry. I can untie shoestrings at night when knots baffle the three youngest. I can read the funnies to the two who haven't learned how to read.

The boss and I are going to begin baking bread. He will do the kneading if I will put in the salt; and I'll bake it if someone will put it in the oven, turn it, and take it out for me. Baker's bread is good for a time, but the homemade kind is better after one tires of eating the other.

I can wash chubby hands and dirt-streaked faces and wipe noses, too—although not very expertly—if their owners happen to be a bit reluctant about cleaning up.

If the dishes weren't so heavy I'd set the table, but it might be best to call one of my assistants from his play to do that. Besides, I can't seem to find anything in the kitchen without help. The specialists out there have begun to complain about my meddling. Last night they couldn't find the butcher knife because I had put it where I used to keep it instead of where *they* keep it. The cupboard and cabinet drawers and doors, like the dishes, seem to be unusually heavy just now. So I'll give up setting the table.

Keeping house and working for one's own family suits me so well that I'm counting on spending all my time (except when I'm busy at the typewriter) at the task by the time spring is here again.

7

At Home on the Farm

As this chapter's columns deal mostly with happenings at home they have been grouped together, although several columns pertaining to other subjects have been scattered among them as they appeared in print.

T H E boss had piled some wood near the back door instead of throwing it in the basement. It was damp, and we thought it would dry off more rapidly in the sunlight.

When the fire became low I hated to face the chilly breezes to get one of the needed chunks. Finally the task couldn't be put off any longer. As I straightened up with my load a boy came running around the house, the wind tousling his hair and whipping his garments tight to his body.

"I locked you out, Mother," he boasted.

Another lad came running down the slope. "He bolted the door, Mother. He bolted the door."

Sure enough, the door was bolted. I put the wood down on the back porch and hurried around to the front door. Of course I was pretty sure—but I thought I'd go see. Yes, the night lock was on. So when the back door was bolted and two boys left by way of the front entrance, they had indeed locked themselves as well as their mother out of the house.

By this time two young gentlemen were quite thoroughly frightened. And chilled. They were positive we'd never see the inside of the house again. Bruce blamed Irvin for fastening the bolt. Irvin argued that it hadn't been necessary for Bruce to follow him outside. Several wild plans were suggested, but neither boy could think of anything that would suit the other.

Meanwhile I shivered and examined the windows until I

found one that had been left unlocked. When I began to take off the screen my escorts offered much advice. They offered to help by hunting a rock or stick with which I could break the pane out of the sash. When the window was up at last I had to boost both boys instead of one over the sill so that the door could be unbolted.

After repairing the fires I hunted my hat and coat before I replaced the screen. More than that, I washed the window while the screen was out. The rest of our windows may be getting pretty dingy, but there is one pane through which we can get a clear view. I know just where the boys will practice their penmanship the next morning we find the windows covered with frost.

B I L L was in a cardboard box in the corner of Grandma's kitchen the first time I saw him. Dean's parents had gone to see some of his mother's relatives that day, and Dean couldn't go off and leave a baby lamb all day so he and the lamb came to Grandma's.

The youngster ate milk out of a bottle every two hours. I didn't approve of Dean's method of feeding him. He took the bottle away before Bill had all he wanted. In answer to my protests the lamb's owner insisted that it wouldn't do to let Bill eat his fill or he would get sick. I expounded upon the way we raised pet lambs—out of a bucket, like feeding a calf, and all they wanted every two hours from the very first. But I'm only an aunt-in-law, and in-laws' opinions seldom count. On the way home I stated my belief that Dean was starving that lamb. Like Dean, I had forgotten that there are a good many successful ways of doing anything if one sticks closely to the method one is following.

The other day Dean brought Bill down to see if he could trade him for a lady lamb. Bill hadn't starved, so I couldn't say, "I told you so." In fact, he is bigger than our own lambs; I can comfort myself by the knowledge that he was an earlier lamb.

Dean tied Bill to a tree and we went across the road to bring in the sheep so that Dean could choose the lamb he wanted for his agriculture work at school. Bill baaed when we left him by the tree. He had seen no sheep since his mother's owner gave him to Dean when he was a few hours old, so William depended upon human companionship; and being left alone in a strange back yard didn't appeal to him.

When the sheep came running across the road Bill didn't

know what to think. The sight of a group of strange-looking creatures rushing toward him filled him with terror. He did not know that he looked like them or that he was bigger than any of them. Billy ran around and around the tree until his rope was wound up, and he could go no farther. He became a little less frightened when he saw that none of the odd animals tried to hurt him. But he didn't trust them.

Bill is in the pasture across the road now, but he isn't with the other sheep. He follows us to the well when we go to pump water, gets his drink, watches the other lambs run back to their favorite feeding places, and comes back with us as far as the gate. He thinks we are cruel because we keep him over there in such a lonely spot when he wants to be in the yard with us and entertain himself by bumping our youngest, who runs and screams when he sees Billy coming toward him.

Passersby may wonder why a very fat young lamb stands at the gate in the hot sun instead of going with the other sheep to the shade of the haystacks or timber. It is because Bill hasn't learned that he is a sheep.

NOVEMBER can be as disagreeable as any month in the year. When we have bad weather at this time it is very unpleasant for both humans and livestock. A cold rain that isn't quite cold enough to be snow chills us much more than a real snow. Then, too, we are not yet accustomed to cold weather so soon after the heat of summer has departed.

Today isn't what we think of as a typical November day, yet I suppose we have as many beautiful days at this season as at any other. No doubt a storm is coming and causing this warm bright day. We appreciate it and the opportunity to make the most of the warm sunshine while we have it.

The canary has taken a bath, gone through a number of intricate calisthenics, and given us music worthy of an orchestra. He pouts when it is cold or cloudy, but he doesn't mind admitting there is some good in the world when the sun warms and brightens things up.

The hired girl is washing windows. The men are making fence posts, trying to keep up with an enormous gang of WPA workers who are moving our fence so a new road can be built. We can't believe it yet. But it must be true, the news we have been hearing for the last two years. Yes, we are to be on a graveled road that will not force us to be stay-at-homes a good share of the year.

The little boys are helping the men. Their enthusiasm makes up for their lack of muscle. It was with regret that the big boys left for school when there are so many interesting things going on at home.

Some thirty new pigs down at the barn keep me running. Before long they will be fairly independent. But just now it is handy to have someone make their mothers get up if they happen to lie down on small, wriggling squealers or step on wee pink feet. It is terrible to get lost in a corner of the pen two or three feet away from the mother pig and the rest of the progeny. Unless I am there to help the wanderer find his way back, all the fussy mothers get up to learn the cause of the pitiful outcry. Then there is a general mix-up during which some small porker is likely to get smashed or crippled.

Two of the youngest members of the porcine family found last night a bit too cold. They are sleeping in a box by the fireplace. They thought it was a good location at first, but now small grunts and whimpers emanate from their refuge. Even if the temperature is just right, no creature can be happy on an empty stomach. I am not very anxious for the job of taking these two speckled youngsters back to the barn. Down there everything is so peaceful at present that I hate to disturb the three sleeping families. But every time the hungry ones drop off to sleep they wake again to become more insistent in their clamor for food.

I'm not doing much good here at the house anyway. The cook has come downstairs to discover I permitted the light bread to get too hot and now part of it is spoiled. I guess I'd better take my livestock and go outside. I can pick up kindling and carry wood into the basement while I'm caring for the pigs. Live creatures, unlike bread, make a fuss about it if things don't go right.

SO many of those who wrote wanted to know what we did at Christmas. There isn't very much to tell, but the boys say we had the nicest Christmas we have ever had.

As usual Santa slipped in on Christmas eve during the supper hour and left our gifts. The two youngest think it was a great joke on me, for he left the things right here in my room and I was napping and didn't see him. No doubt the old fellow was very busy this year, for everything was in the wrappers just as they had come from the store. It kept Grandma busy for a while picking up discarded wrapping paper and price tags. Before everything had been inspected it was necessary to take the new train and the buses into the living room where there would be more room for them to run.

While there was a temporary lull in the uproar, a telephone call was made to my brother's house two miles away. Santa hadn't been there yet, so there was much excitement in two households as the small girls who were anxiously waiting and the boys who had their toys already made wild guesses as to his whereabouts.

On Christmas morning my brother, his daughters, my sister, and her husband picked up my mother and brought their gifts to us. Mamma had dressed a chicken the previous afternoon, so the boss cooked it, with dumplings, for our Christmas dinner. In the afternoon my cousin and her husband came to see us—the first visit we have had since last May.

On Sunday Dick's two nephews came in the car for the boys and took them up to Grandma's to their Christmas tree and dinner. They saw Santa Claus, which was quite an event in the lives of the two youngest. It was their first view of the old gentleman, who asked some embarrassing questions. Bruce explained after he arrived home that he told him he had been a good boy because he is good more than he is naughty. When the question was put to Irvin he evaded it with diplomacy. That boy would make a good president. Instead of answering, he remarked, "I'd 'gather' have *that* truck." So Santa handed over the toy to the three-year-old diplomat and went on to one of the small cousins.

ON the way home from town we stopped at the brickyard and filled the back seat of the car with tile, 141 of them, for tiling out the spring.

After we picked up the rest of the family at Grandma's, the front seat was loaded about as heavily as the back. The driver held Bruce, I held the baby, and the two big boys took up the remaining space. It didn't take long to travel the remaining three miles, but we were glad when our cramped ride was over.

The men at once unloaded the tile into the wagon and set out for the spring. The ground isn't frozen much yet in the shelter of the trees, but at any time we can expect real winter that will stop such work as digging trenches for tile. We are anxious to run the water into a tank for the stock. As it is, we are afraid some of the cattle might be pushed out onto the ice and drown, as one of our cows did some fourteen winters ago. It isn't easy to tile water out of a spring that runs into the creek bed. It would be a lesser problem if the spring outlet were higher up on the steep bank instead of at the very foot of it. They are hoping to finish the work today.

Probably our tenant on the other farm will bring a truckload of grain. Somebody will have to go the half mile from here to the spring to call Dick so he can help with the unloading. That will make some delay in the work there as well as in the housework.

The mumpy one, virtually well but weak and unsuccessful in a half-hearted attempt to recover his usual good nature, is quite busy reading one of his Christmas books. The two youngest scarcely have time to eat. The new cloth dogs, the red fire truck, and the green one require much attention at present. As yet the other gifts have received only a cursory notice.

There is the weekly cleaning, mending, and another newspaper column to be done. But it keeps me busy tying the dogs' neckties, settling disputes that arise when the owners of the dogs interrupt the book reader, fixing fires, and answering the telephone.

This is the long winter of which we read, when the farm family rests, reads, chats, and listens to the radio while waiting for spring to come so they can begin work again. Yes, it is winter, but I haven't noticed any difference in the amount of work to be done. In that respect it is just the same as March, July, or October so far as I can tell.

M OTHER, I'm ready to go outside now."

"You can't go. It's raining."

"Mother, I'm going to take these rifle shells outside, Mother. I'm going to take these rifle shells out to the sandpile. Put sand in them. Mother, put my coat on me."

"You can't go outside. It's too cold and rainy. See the puddles of water out there?"

"Mother, I'm going to take these rifle shells out to the sandpile. Mother, I'd rather go out to the sandpile now. Mother, I'd rather have my coat. I want to take these rifle shells and put sand in them."

Mother groans and sits down at desk.

"Milk, milk, milk! I'm milking a cow."

"Here, here! You musn't do that. You will spoil the milk pail."

"Oh, I didn't know it would hurt the old milk pail to hit it with the checkerboard. I guess I'll go to town."

"I'd rather go to town, too. Get over. Move the milk bucket over. I want in that box, too. I'm going to town, too."

"Honk, honk. Move this bucket over there. Put the boards in it."

"No, no. You're going the wrong way. I'd rather go this way."

"No, town's over this way. There wouldn't be any town over that way."

"Oh."

"Honk, honk br-br-br-z-z-z-z. Honk, honk."

"I'd rather go this way."

"We are going that way."

"Oh."

"Roll the windows up. It's dinnertime. I'm hungry. Let's stop and buy something to eat. Throw the boards out. I'm 'King X' now. This board is a sandwich."

"It's raining now."

"I'm a baseball player. Ole King Cole was a very ole soldier. This bucket is my hat."

"No. It's my hat. A merry ole soul, a merry ole soul, a merry ole. . . ."

"Here, give it to me. You don't know how to wear this kind of a hat."

"Give it back. I want it back."

"Oh, all right. But wear it so when you get down in the ground the soldiers can shoot at you."

"Bruce, put the milk bucket away. Bruce, put the milk bucket away. Bruce, put this milk bucket away, Bruce."

"Mother, have you got time to play a game of dummies with me?"

THREE or four weeks ago the boys brought *Little Women* home from the school library for me to read. But I didn't read it right away. There was something more important to demand my attention at the time. One day the boys asked me if I had finished it, so they could take it back. I hadn't even started it. There was no particular hurry to take it back, for our school is so small that nobody was likely to want it to read. Yet we hated to keep it too long, even though nothing was said by the other school patrons.

It was with some reluctance that I opened the book one evening. I was afraid that I might be a little disappointed in finding it less interesting than I had in the days when I read and reread it so much. But I'm glad I've started reading it again. It is different this time. It tells me a different story. I no longer feel

cheated because I never knew Meg, Jo, Beth, and Amy. The story
makes me want to see the little girls that Cleo, Grace, and Bertie
used to be. The March girls had no more adventures than we had
during our school days together. Of course, in the book time
traveled more rapidly and we could read a year of their lives in
a few hours. A year of our own lives seemed a long while to us
then. It doesn't now.

The chapter I read last night while I was waiting to take the
light bread out of the oven so I could go to bed made me think
of the period just after country school days were over. I was
almost homesick for Martha, Ruth, and the others who went
through the foolish, adventurous teens with me. Martha (she's a
grandma now) and Ruth live a short ten or twelve miles from
here. Yet I see them only a little more often than Cleo, Grace, and
Bertie who live so far away.

It is odd that I see so many things in the story that I didn't
see twenty-five years ago. It seemed quite perfect to me then,
even though I missed part of it somehow. It makes me want to
see the friends I have not seen since that day in 1922 when my
own school days ended. At that time it didn't seem possible that
sixteen years could pass without seeing Helen, Irene, Floy, Dag-
mar, and all the rest. How I'd like to see them and talk over our
silly pranks. A few years ago I heard that Helen lived in Chicago
and Irene in Hollywood. I haven't heard from any of them for
years.

To a young girl, *Little Women* is a story of a group of interesting girls. To a grown woman, the book is a story of her own
girlhood. I'm glad I'm reading it again and that I find it even
more entrancing than I did the first time.

Two more members of our family had operations in
1938. However, Charles and Bruce did not go to the hospital. Their
tonsils were removed in the doctor's house in Blakesburg.

A N Y names that I may mention while under the influence
of ether will be entirely fictitious and will not be pertaining
to and are not to be considered as a reflection upon any
living being." So stated our second son the evening before his
tonsil operation. Having been a potential patient myself, I quite
understand how he could be somewhat nervous when he wondered what conversational subjects he might choose when not
quite himself.

My problem of the moment was somewhat different. How were we to manage to feed the other members of the family the next morning and yet induce the six-year-old to do without a drink or breakfast? He has a habit of arising at 4 A.M. while the two sons who were not to lose their tonsils are sleepyheads who like to stay up late at night and arise very late the next morning. However, the two who were to undergo the operation were somewhat excited the last evening. Charles was a bit shaky and his younger brother, Bruce, was almost overcome with pride to think he was going to receive so much attention. They couldn't get to sleep very early.

The next morning Dick and I ate alone. Then Vaughn was aroused for his breakfast. Finally the almost impossible feat of getting the youngest downstairs without awakening the other two was accomplished. Charles and Bruce slept late, although we hadn't even dared hope for such good fortune. When at last they opened their eyes, Charles who knew breakfast and drinks were forbidden stayed in bed and thought of amusing things to entertain his younger brother. They arose when we told them it was time to get ready to go to town. We hurried to collect blankets, pillows, and everything that we were to take with us.

The boss didn't try to shave. Two days previously a horse had kicked him, and one of the kicks had been in his mouth. He wasn't feeling like shaving or going with us, either. But Irvin didn't think it would be at all fair for him to stay at home, so Dick took him and went as far as my mother's house and the eldest took us to town.

Before we reached our destination the fumes of ether reached us. As we climbed out of the car we glanced across the street where a blanket-wrapped youngster was being carried in at the front door of his home. He hadn't had far to go for his operation.

Clutching our pillows and blankets, we climbed the steps. On the porch a very miserable lad, his eyes red rimmed from weeping, sat stolidly in a chair. He had balked and could not be induced to enter the building. One of our sons could have his turn.

Each wanted to be first, but I had promised Bruce that morning, so Charles waited. I stayed with Bruce while he manfully breathed deep, got a bit frightened, calmed down again, and went to sleep. Then I hurried back to help the other boy get ready. Just as Charles dropped off to sleep, I heard wails from the waking Bruce and had to rush off to his bedside as he came back to consciousness. That was one time the doctor had no bother from a frantic parent. I was much too busy to bother him.

It seemed a long time before Charles was brought down from the operating room to the bed next to the one in which Bruce was tossing. In fact, I was quite convinced that he hadn't lived through the operation and that they were not going to let me know it until Bruce was better, so I would be less distressed about the younger lad. Aren't we parents silly? It was a relief to have him brought to me. He talked, but all the names he mentioned were those of his three brothers, which was a great disappointment to one of his schoolmates who was helping care for the rows of patients.

This is the third day. Bruce is well enough to play part of the time. Our long-legged cook and housekeeper isn't recovering quite that rapidly. Evidently our meals are to be skimpy and the house unkempt for some time yet, which doesn't matter at all. There will be plenty to eat when the boys are well again.

CHARLES, eleven years old, is up after several days in bed. As was to be expected, he is spending his time in the library. That suits the two youngest. They, too, like nothing better than books.

Doubtless Vaughn has a warmer spot in his heart for school and reading than he will admit. So although he does a good bit of pacing about while he is a shut-in, he has managed to pass away a good many hours with books and magazines when his eyes will permit that pleasure. The whooping cough is gone but the after-effects linger. So with the other boys Vaughn is spending the afternoon looking over the bookshelves. He hasn't found anything to read yet. Probably that is because he keeps looking over the shoulder of Charles, who is looking at a huge geography so heavy that it has to have a chair of its own.

Your farm woman will have to admit that she herself spent more time talking with them about the old maps than any housekeeper ought to waste on a busy afternoon. Perhaps the map of Louisiana drawn in 1784 was the most interesting of all. On this map the Missouri and Mississippi rivers are much too far apart. Iowa is not so wide as that. But no doubt the explorers who drew the map didn't see all the country.

The part of Louisiana that is now southern Iowa and northern Missouri is designated as Extensive Meadows Full of Buffaloes. This region included all the territory between the Missouri and the Moingona rivers. From the location of the last-named river it must be the one now called the Des Moines. So all these old buffalo wallows we see in sheltered spots in our pastures were once occupied by real, live buffaloes.

And for those of us who are interested in the old Indian graves there are pictures of the people of that time. One is of the people who lived on the east side of the Mississippi and another is of those who lived on the west. Somehow I doubt if the artist who made those engravings ever saw a woman of either of the tribes he pictured. I'll bet no early American female ever wore a low necked, ruffled-sleeved creation with a tail like a man's shirt and a top like Grandma's nightgown. However, he had a right to use his imagination. It wasn't very likely that the readers of the book would ever see Louisiana.

The greater part of the information came from those who had actually seen this country. But I know they didn't visit the northern part of the Louisiana Territory during January or February. Or if they did the weather has changed greatly since this region became Minnesota, the Dakotas, Iowa, and Nebraska. To quote the book, "In winter there are only heavy rains, without any nipping frosts."

But who am I to laugh about a little mistake such as that? The book was interesting to its readers 150 years ago. It is absorbing nowadays. What more could any author ask?

THE Urbana Booster 4-H Club met here last night. Several of the boys could not attend because of the muddy roads. That shows how good I am as a weather prophet. I had predicted a blizzard would postpone the meeting. Nobody was surprised but me because I was the only one looking for it.

When I was small we used to ask one of the neighbors what kind of weather we were going to have and when he told us his opinion we expected the opposite. Probably he guessed wrong purposely part of the time to keep his record intact. I'm just as good at guessing wrong as he was.

This morning is the same as all other mornings after the club has met. The four lads in this household are not accustomed to losing sleep. The youngest never loses any sleep; when his bedtime comes he goes to sleep no matter where he may be or how much of interest there is to see.

The six-year-old is different. He never did like this thing of going to bed. Not being modern parents who do things as they should be done, we were not quite smart enough to get him to bed at 6 P.M. when he was small. Even before he could walk we went to bed and he played about in the dark, having a good time by himself. The first time I awoke in the night I hunted him, picked

him up from where he had fallen asleep, and put him to bed. He
acquired the habit of waking in the night and climbing up on the
high side of his bed and falling off. After that I made a bed of
folded comforters for him on the floor. As usual, he was the last
to go to bed last night although it was 11 P.M. instead of his
customary bedtime. This morning he alternates between sitting
on the floor very near the fireplace and lying on the couch.

His next eldest brother insists that he isn't going to school,
which disgusts the eldest completely. It doesn't take much to
disgust Vaughn after he has lost two hours sleep.

The big folks of the family seem somewhat tired and cross
themselves, although they slept late enough to make up for getting to bed somewhat later. I don't think they lost enough sleep
to matter. This caring for three boys who do feel their loss of
sleep is making them tired. The youngest is the only cheerful one
in the family. I think we are mighty lucky to have a youngest.

WELL, I've joined the Wednesday club. I forgot my
handbag—probably there was no money in it anyway—
so I didn't pay my dues. But my name is on the secre-
tary's list with the rest of them. This isn't the first time I've
joined clubs and things. I knew better, but they asked me and I
joined.

The other times there was the rush to hurry through the
work in order to get ready to go and afterward another rush to
attempt catching up on neglected duties. Finally, even I could see
that there wasn't room in my life for club work and I'd have to
give it up.

This time there wasn't an opportunity to think things over
before I went. I did that last night after I went to bed. But when
they telephoned me Tuesday evening I forgot about the other
times. It seemed like a good idea. I never see the neighbors. This
would be a good way to renew acquaintances. So Wednesday
morning I hurried through what had to be written, picked the
lettuce and pulled the onions for dinner, made a good many trips
to the nests of the hens that were hatching, helped Charles do the
weekly washing, cooked the meal, brought in the garments that
were dry enough to iron, put the new chicks in the brooder house,
washed my face, combed the tangles out of my hair, donned a
clean dress, put on my hat, brought in some more of the wash
that had dried, and went to the meeting.

They elected me president. Right then I began to think of

some of the reasons why I should have stayed home. But I can't blame them. It was self-defense. There is only one way to muzzle club members who are inclined to chatter about anything and nothing. If they are given something to do, they have to keep comparatively quiet.

This way I'll be kept busy curbing the other talkative members who are reminded of choice bits of gossip in the midst of the regular program. Since I'm the worst of all, it is quite an accomplishment to have silenced me. That is, if they have; the plan may not work.

Having been a mother for well onto fourteen years I had thought that nothing could surprise me any more. But when I arrived back home it seemed incredible that one house could be so muddy as this one. It didn't seem possible that so many unfolded newspapers could be on one table or so many things on the floor instead of in their accustomed places. I spent the night pondering these and other matters. Just how was I going to manage the ironing and the other things I didn't do yesterday— the cleaning, the mending, and everything else?

But I belong to the Wednesday club. Probably I'll be sorry. I'm not of the efficient type who can feed the family and keep the house immaculate in spite of being at home only when there is nowhere to go. No doubt the club will be sorry, for I'm not one of those praiseworthy creatures who is seen and not heard.

However, it is pleasant to contemplate at present when only one half day's work has been postponed. It is muddier than ever again today. Maybe I'll do the ironing and other things and let the cleaning go until tomorrow.

T HE old woman who lived in a shoe wasn't any busier than the boys of this family have been recently. When two caterpillar tractors drawing road-building outfits came to cut down the big hill and grade up the road ready for its all-weather surface, it didn't take the boss and me long to learn that we couldn't expect a whole lot of help from our assistants while so much of interest was going on in our vicinity.

It is difficult for a lad to cut weeds, pick up cobs and sticks, wash dishes, or milk cows when there is so much for him to see. Oddly enough he can work at marvelous engineering feats with machinery of his own construction, pull the wagon with its home-made trailer carrying the long-suffering cat or puppy, or read the comic pages and forget all about the caterpillar climbing up and down steep banks and going through the same maneuvers that had hindered him at chore time. Young farmers, like their parents, go through times when duties pile up so rapidly that sometimes they wonder if things will run smoothly ever again.

Acquiring a new pup who demands much attention and receives more and then the building of the new road would seem to be about all four boys could handle in one season. But Dorothy, the lame duck, was thoughtless enough to become broody. She is determined to set in a down-lined nest she has built in the shade of a clump of buckbrush.

Several momentous questions have arisen. Shall Dorothy be given a setting of hen eggs or would it be best to pile some boards in her nest in an attempt to discourage her broody tendencies? How much would a setting of duck eggs cost? How many duck eggs make a setting? How many hen eggs would make a setting for a duck? Would she claim small brown eggs instead of large white ones? Would they be easy for a clumsy old duck to break? Would she want the little chicks after they hatched? Would she try to make them swim? Would the nest be in the sunshine at any time during the day so that Dorothy, not so young as she was six or eight years ago, might be overcome by heat?

Dorothy's predicament was forgotten when five small kittens were discovered in an unused manger in the barn. Each boy has taken it upon himself to see that the other three do not harm the baby cats. Of course it would not do any harm for him to look at them a little to see why they have no eyes and to learn what they would do if taken an inch or so away from the nest so they couldn't find each other. But he knows better than to trust his brothers who are so rough. Torn between his desire to fondle the wee squirmers and his fear that the other boys will harm them, each lad is too excited to be of much use at farm work.

I'm glad I'm a woman with only cooking, housework, hoeing, canning, berrypicking, milking, and a few little things like that to do instead of being a boy with so many worries.

AN unnatural quiet has settled over the house. That may be the reason for the ringing in my head and ears. More likely, though, the queer feeling is just an echo of the shouts that have been resounding through these rooms until some thirty seconds ago.

Just before all the noise stopped, I heard much thumping of the loose floorboards in the attic. Then four lads descended with their latest find. They are going to make a kite out of some of the loot they were carrying. All talking at once, they stopped to explain what a good kite it would be. Then they went out to the shop to make the remarkable craft, which will soon be soaring aloft I am led to believe. Each of them has made a trip or two back to the house for more materials while I have been writing. The head carpenter is silent, although I can hear the other three voices. No doubt the speechless one has the hammer in his hand and his tongue between his teeth.

But although there are no boys in the house it would require only a very little detective work to prove that school is out and that the first day of vacation is being enjoyed to the utmost.

The floor in the library is littered with blocks, toys, wheels, spools, and other treasures that belong to the two youngest. The box in which these things belong is in the middle bedroom. By its side rests a pair of scuffed shoes, one with a hole in it. Bruce is going barefoot this warm day. On my bed I see a storybook, the segments of a map puzzle, and the box that is supposed to contain the map. There are a cap and a magazine on the dresser. Blocks, checkers, dominoes, and two homemade Rook decks adorn the rug in the living room. The carom board rests on the sofa. Chairs are grouped according to the way they were needed while some game was played or as they were pushed back out of the way to make room for four boys who needed to be on the floor.

It is impossible to walk anywhere without stepping on marbles.

The kite-building has stopped while three boys are hunting for the paste. Let us hope they do not find too many other things in their search. As usual, they will become quite weary when I suggest that it might be a good idea to do a bit of picking up and moving things back where they belong. So the more spoils they bring out, the more cleaning up will need to be done.

Irvin is on the dining room couch cutting a piece of paper into very small pieces. I can see where he will be stricken with a headache very suddenly when time comes to pick up the paper. The scissors have changed hands. Now I'll have to pick up the paper myself. Neither boy would want to tire himself by picking up the bits the other cut. Each of them will be sure he didn't do much of it himself.

If they decide to go to the sandpile after a while, I'll try to remember to hide the colored crayons. Those marks on the glass of the front door, the screen, and the porch post do not appeal to my defective sense of the artistic. But first I must go hunt that paste before the contents of every drawer and shelf in the kitchen and bathroom are put into worse disorder than usual.

MOTHER, Mother, what are you going to do?"
"Move the curio cabinet while the big boys are home to help."
"Where? Where are you going to move it, Mother? Well, I didn't know you kept the key there. I've been wanting to find it. Let me—what's this? I want to eat those hickory nuts. What made them so big? I want to eat them."
"They wouldn't be good. They are too old."
"How old?"
"They've been in there as long as I can remember. Probably they are older than I."
"That would be pretty old, wouldn't it, Mother? Where did you get these honey locust thorns? Look—at these. Are they good to eat?"
"No, they are buckeyes. They are poison."
"I want those moccasins."
"Is that a buffalo horn?"
"Just see all the gold in these rocks. Why don't we sell some of it? It would bring about a million dollars. Wouldn't you rather have a million dollars, Mother?"
"What are these and these and these?"
"Don't all ask questions at once. Those are petrified fish vertebrae, and those are petrified snail shells."
"Is this petrified rice, Mother?"
"No, those are bits of shells and rocks. Will one of you bring me a dustcloth?"
"I had one the other day but I can't remember where I put it, Mother."
"What's in this bottle?"
"Dirt from Carolina."
"Dirt isn't that color. Where is the Wind Cave? It says Wind Cave on that rock. Mother—Mother—it says 'picked up in Portland, Maine,' on this rock, Mother."
"Mother, how would you like to walk on this stuff without any shoes? That would hurt, wouldn't it, Mother? Why are some of these arrowheads big and some of them little? Did the little boys shoot the little ones and the big boys shoot the middle-size ones? Do you suppose some old Indian killed somebody with this big one? Its point is broken off. Do you suppose that was what broke it?"

"How would you like a big old eagle to pick you up with a lot of claws like this and carry you off? That would hurt, wouldn't it, Mother?"

"Who broke all of these rattlesnake rattles?"

"I didn't, Mother. I didn't. It wasn't me."

"Let me see them. I never saw them, so I couldn't break them, could I, when I didn't even—I didn't want you to put them away."

"Mother, I can't find the dustcloth anywhere. I'll look downstairs."

"Help me carry this first."

"Oh, boy, that's where you are going to put it, isn't it? I'll carry things back. I'll be careful. I'll be—what's this?"

"Mother, I can't find a dustcloth down here either."

"Here is one. Why don't you boys go play a while."

"We want to help you, Mother."

"Mother, let's sell some of this gold. It's worth $10 an ounce."

"I don't think all of that is gold. It isn't the right color. Some of it is mica, silver, lead, copper, and other metals. It is just ore and not very valuable."

"What is in this bottle?"

"A tarantula."

"A ter—ter—Whee! Lookit his legs! Get outa my way! You hadn't ought to try to carry this stuff, anyway. You might break something. Mother, you better watch him. Here, I wanta see that."

"There now. That's everything. Where are you going to put the key this time, Mother?"

OF late it has become increasingly difficult to find new locations to hide the curio cabinet key. It will no longer do to put it in a vase, or on a nail behind a picture. On the top of the door casing seemed like a good place. Our youngest is very tall for his age, but even though he climbed upon a chair and tiptoed it was out of his reach.

Like a good many others I am not so wise as I believe in my most egotistical moments. How was I to know what Charles, who promises to become the tallest member of our family, would do? He took the key down. When he put it back, he shoved it down behind the casing before he noticed what he was doing.

With the key behind a strip of thoroughly dry walnut, nailed with six nails—I counted them—to studdings of thoroughly dry oak and honey locust, what are we going to tell the boss when he gets home from work? Shall we keep quiet about it until a logical moment comes to break the news? Or shall we tell him at once? He is not going to relish the task of tearing off that casing, ruining it in the process, and finding another to take its place.

The cause of our predicament suggested that it might be pulled out with a magnet, but we have no magnet small enough to slip back there. We tried fishing with the butcher knife but had no success worth mentioning. Perhaps Dick or Vaughn may be able to figure out some way to accomplish our purpose without doing any wrecking. Both are good at engineering tasks we less gifted members of the family have no idea how to do. The two youngest are quite interested. They have offered several suggestions, such as taking an ax and chopping the house down, pounding on the wall with a hammer to see if the key will fall out, and the like. None of these has seemed practical. But neither have the ideas of their mother and big brother.

The lad who put the key where it now is does not relish the task of informing his dad and big brother about the occurrence. He couldn't do as one of my cousins did when he broke the mouthpiece off the telephone transmitter. The culprit stuck the broken mouthpiece back where it belonged. When my uncle went to the telephone that evening he put his hand on the transmitter and the mouthpiece came off in his hand. He thought he had broken it himself, and the other members of the family thought it was very funny. But there wouldn't be any way to make Dick or Vaughn think they were to blame in this. Charles will just have to wait until he collects enough courage to confess what happened.

Meanwhile, I'll have one less worry. No longer is there any danger that our two young explorers may gain access to the interior of the curio cabinet.

THE county agent was giving instructions to a group of men who were to call on a number of farmers to acquire some information about farming practices. "If the men are not at home, don't ask their wives," he said. "Few women know anything about the farm, and they'll not tell you." Then as an afterthought he added, "And don't ask the boy. He'll tell you too much."

That reminded me of something that happened here during that hot July we had two years ago. A group of workmen came every day to drink and to fill their water jugs. We didn't know just where they were working or what they were doing. If they had been working near here we would have known it. We wondered how it happened that they didn't get their drinking water nearer their place of work. One day our eldest was here when they arrived. Boylike, he accompanied them to the well to listen to the conversation and ask a few questions if given an opportunity.

After they left he reported all that had been said. First, each of the young men took a long drink and made a remark about how good and cold the water was. One of them asked Vaughn what was the matter with this neighborhood that everybody had cisterns instead of wells.

"This," he stated emphatically, "is the only good water around here. At every other place we have gone they have cisterns. I just can't bear to drink cistern water."

"Nor can I." "Or I," echoed his companions.

Vaughn told them all he knew. He hasn't yet learned the wisdom of keeping silent when it is best to permit people to be happy through ignorance. Many a passing traveler has given us compliments about our good drinking water and gone on his way without knowing he had been drinking rainwater. But the eldest showed these men where the tile ran under the ground to bring the rainwater into the well after it had run off the barn roof and into the filter.

The men took their jugs and left. They never came after any more water. They had been getting much enjoyment out of their good cold drinks for a week. No doubt the water acquired a terrible flavor and aroma as soon as they learned its source.

THE boys are having a little vacation from housework this week. Their grandmother is spending a few days with us. It is fun to help Grandma with the dishes and to peel the potatoes for her. It is work when they do it by themselves. She arrived just as one boy was having a terrible struggle with the pillowcases he was ironing. He was glad to let her iron the white clothes for him while he finished the everyday shirts and other colored things.

An agent who came on washday told them he and his brother did the family washing for years when they were boys. That was a comfort to the boys of this family. They do not mind doing the housework during their mother's recuperation, but it is a bit of worry to them lest people criticize them for doing girls' work.

They are somewhat proud of their ability to cook. They haven't acquired much skill at eggbeating and sometimes their cakes sink a little in the center. But cooking is more fun than dishes, dusting, sweeping, or keeping the tables and mantle tidy.

Bedmaking is the one task that is too much for them. However, their mother needs some exercise even if she is too weak this summer to do much other work. So she makes the beds while they are doing the breakfast dishes.

When school begins next fall—and that time is not far away—we are going to miss our willing but clumsy cooks, housekeepers, and laundrymen. Maybe the youngest will be my chief assistant when his brothers are at school.

Just now Grandma and Irvin are mopping the floor. There isn't much danger that I shall have to do any mopping this next fall and winter unless I get particular and decide I want the dust under the cupboard, cabinet, stove, and other furniture mopped up. When Irvin mops he scrubs with all his might, but he doesn't hit the corners or out-of-the-way spots unless it is by accident. He did mop under the desk just now. Probably that was because it gave him an opportunity to order his mother to get away so she wouldn't be in his road.

It is nice to be able to take a summer vacation with nothing to do but writing, mending, bedmaking, and a few little tasks that are easy for feminine hands but too difficult and intricate for small boys.

A T last our five-year-old Bruce is a proud schoolboy. Irvin would be a schoolboy too, if he had anything to say about it. It was a heartbreaking time for him when his bigger brother started off and left him there. He cried—and when he cries he does his very best—for an hour and forty-five minutes. It seemed much longer than that, but I looked at the clock to make sure that it was running. When at last there were no more tears to flow, the outburst ceased almost as suddenly as it had begun.

It was a very quiet small boy who followed me about the house the rest of the morning. After the noon meal he donned his outdoor wraps and helped build a fire and carry water for the butchering. The second morning he felt very important when he explained that he couldn't go to school because he had to stay home and help make sausage. The third morning he took no notice of the departure of his brothers, only stopping his play long enough to fetch the dinner pail from the kitchen. Then with a hasty good-bye he went back to his toys.

Probably he is beginning to learn that a badly spoiled lad of three can have more fun playing alone than with a group of brothers who do not altogether approve of his selfishness. Usually he has his own way, so when they rebel he thinks he is greatly abused.

Thank you to the readers who wrote about curing meat and selling popcorn. My sympathy to the one who had to write with a pencil because her three-year-old "fixed" her fountain pen for her when he heard her complain that something was the matter with it. I know just how she feels. Once my brother and my husband decided my fountain pen wasn't working properly. I insisted that it was quite good enough for me, but no mere woman can make headway in an argument with two men. It didn't seem necessary to use my favorite nail file to repair the pen either. But I was overruled. The repair work took an hour or two. When it was completed I had no fountain pen, nor any nail file, either.

BRUCE remarked last night that he was glad the school week was ended. He thought it would be nice to spend Saturday helping his dad take care of the little lambs. It is wonderful to get to go to school, to learn words, and to count and write. Of course, he is not jealous but it does make him feel odd to come home late in the afternoon and small brother tells about the work he and Dad did during the day. He went to bed early last night, so he could get in a big day's work helping Dad today. Irvin has been looking forward to Saturday too. He has told me several times that he was going to have Bruce write words for him all day.

However, now that Saturday is here the lambs do not seem to be getting much attention. There haven't been any inquiries for pencils and paper, either. After breakfast the two youngest donned their wraps and went to the sandpile. No doubt they were getting ready to sow oats or make garden, for they seemed to be building a fence. At least they were setting stick posts. They didn't work hard enough to stop talking, though. I could hear a steady chatter as I went about my work. The week they had been separated has been a long one for them. There is much for each to tell the other about what happened while one was at school and the other was "helping" Dad.

After a while the big tractor and grader came along to spread the new gravel on the hill in front of the house. Bruce and Irvin came and sat on the bench on the front porch to watch. Presently the gravel was spread, so no motor cars will have to have help getting up the hill in muddy weather. The grader went on to spread the gravel that has been dumped along the road between the railway track and the church. Another road that is treacherous in bad weather now has an all-weather surface.

The boys came into the house to see the comic pages of the newspapers. The mail arrived two hours ago, but they had been too busy with their outdoor duties to come and see about it. One lad is emptying the toybox. Soon the floor will be strewn with blocks, small trucks, and toy tractors. This is going to seem like the days before Bruce became a student. Quite probably we'll hear some terrific quarreling and be required to stop some dreadful fights before the day is over.

So far today, though, the two boys have been too glad to be together to think about disagreeing about anything. We've had a peaceful morning. I hope that we may get through the entire day without any serious differences of opinion. I guess it is good for brothers to be separated part of the time so that they can find out how much they really think of each other.

SOMETIMES it takes a long time to find the motley Jersey cow that we milk, so I didn't want to take Irvin with me on the long tramp over the hills and through the timber. Given his choice of going to the cornfield where his dad was picking corn or to the schoolhouse to meet the first grader, the lad decided to go to the cornfield.

As we passed the barn I saw Ted inside. Why not ride? I'm not much of a jockey, but I was pretty sure I could stay on him if I could manage to mount. By climbing upon the wagon tongue and scrambling from there to Ted's back I made the ascent with little difficulty. Possibly I wasn't very graceful about it, but I reached my goal.

The youngest crept under the cornfield gate and started toward the other end of the field.

Walking as slowly and carefully as he did when the two youngest boys first started to ride, Ted made his way down the path. In no direction could any cattle be seen. The previous night they had been over by the spring, so we headed in that direction. My steed was so sure his rider was about to fall off that all my efforts to induce him to trot failed. The late afternoon air was chilly to my bare hands, so I held the reins in one hand and warmed the other on Ted's neck. Maybe that was one reason he thought I was in danger of falling.

Presently a plaintive voice from the middle of the cornfield announced that Dad could not be found. About that time Dick shouted, and I saw him standing up in the wagon motioning for me to go south instead of west. Turning, I started back. A sobbing small boy ran out of the field toward me. Dick called to him, but his own loud wails drowned out the sound of his dad's voice. It took a good quarter hour to convince him that he could not go with me, and that his other parent could be found if he would stop weeping and look where I was pointing.

By that time I was thoroughly chilled. I wasn't any warmer by the time I had ridden to the opposite corner of the 160 where the cattle were grazing. Ted's gait did not change except when we went down a hill or creek bank. Then he walked more slowly than ever, as if he half expected me to slide over his head at any moment. Mot, the motley cow, was easy to start homeward but she had her own idea of the best route to travel. My unkind remarks made no impression on her and Ted was too afraid of unseating me to trot fast enough to head her off as he does when Vaughn rides him; so we didn't go half a mile east and half a mile north to the house. We came straight down the thickly timbered hill in a beeline for the barn.

When I climbed off his back Ted heaved a great sigh of relief. He hadn't wanted the task of trying to keep me there while we went through the brushes and the brambles and down that steep hillside. Since it is almost perpendicular it really isn't very far down the hill. It took only a few moments to descend in spite of the underbrush, fallen logs, and low hung branches that impeded our progress. But in that period of time I collected all the beggar-lice my garments could hold.

Once down in the valley I could have climbed upon Ted via one of the huge tree stumps and ridden to the barnyard. But I was so cold that I was too hurried to ride. I walked and arrived sooner. It took almost as long to pick the beggar-lice off my coat and stockings as it did to warm my cold hands and feet.

WITH books and paper before him and his pencil in his hand, Vaughn appeared to be getting his English lesson. However, the greater portion of the sheet of paper was blank. The noise and antics of his younger brothers were of more interest to the student than a list of tiresome sentences. Dick was gone and the boys behave just as we did at home when our dad was away.

Presently my mother and I went out on the front porch, thinking that the three younger boys would follow and leave the eldest to wrestle with the stubborn sentences. We had guessed correctly. Out in the bright moonlight there was less boisterousness. We tried to answer the questions about the stars and planets that were fired at us. Gradually we began to realize that the dogs were barking at something. While Charles went to investigate, I went inside to pass my opinion on the finished sentences.

"Mother, come out here. The dogs have a coon or something treed on the telephone pole," came the call from the outside. Vaughn forgot about his lessons and ran with me across the road to where his grandmother and brothers were gathered around the pole. The barking increased in volume now that Nig and Skippy thought assistance was at hand. As my eyes became accustomed to the partial darkness, I distinguished the head of the crouching creature on the pole. It seemed much too large to be a raccoon, but the lighter circles around the eyes convinced me that the others were right.

With my permission, Vaughn ran to the house for the rifle and then yelled back for Charles, who has waited on his big brother ever since he was old enough to walk, to bring the lamp so he could find the ammunition.

Meanwhile, I circled the pole. That took longer than one might think since I had to climb over two gates and through a wire fence to do so. Having been away from the lamp long enough that I could see better, I began to doubt the identity of the object that so infuriated the dogs. There was a head in front of the lighter portion that I had thought encircled the raccoon's eyes; the light color was a ring of white around the animal's neck.

The arrival of the gun caused the barking to become so much louder that I had to shout to make the others acquainted with my discovery. Disappointed at finding no chicken thief to shoot, Vaughn called the dogs by running back across the road and into the yard on a hunt for imaginary rabbits.

Calling "Kitty, kitty," I was rewarded by an answering "Mew," and Tom, Irvin's treasured possession, clambered down from his high perch. Whether it was the moon or our imagination that magnified a very ordinary cat to such magnificent proportions is more than I can tell.

8

Pine Tree Hill

The late 1930s and early 1940s were eventful years in the Faber family. Vaughn and Charles started to high school in the fall of 1938. Bruce had started to grade school in 1937 and Irvin began school in 1939. This chapter consists of a selection of columns from those years.

O N E of our newer readers has asked about the house in which our family lives. It is located on a 240-acre farm of hills, woods, and valley. A crushed rock road runs north and south. On the east side of the road are 80 acres of pastureland. The only buildings there are a corncrib and a sheep shed.

The house is located on the northeast corner of the 160 acres west of the road. It is a little house, twenty-four feet wide and thirty-two feet long. From the north it appears to be a one-story house, as it really is. Only three windows are on this side of the house. From the south it appears to be two stories, since the basement opens at ground level. On this side are three upper windows, with the back porch underneath the middle one and a window on either side of it.

At the west end are two upstairs windows and three basement windows, one each for the kitchen, bathroom, and laundry room. At the east end there is the front door in the middle and one window north of it. The porch covers both the door and window. Underneath the porch is a window to make the furnace room lighter; to the south of it there is another small basement window in the stairway.

North of the house lies the garden. The chicken house is northwest of the house, the cistern is at the northwest corner, and the well is a few feet south of the back porch.

Now for the inside of the house. Both stairways are at the

east end of the house, one directly over the other. The dining room, which contains our fireplace, is in the southeast corner of the basement, and one leads upstairs from the southeast corner of the room. Just over it is the living room. The kitchen is in the southwest corner of the basement, and over it is a bedroom. There is no outside kitchen door. The back door opens into the dining room, near the door into the kitchen.

The bathroom is cut out of the northwest corner of the kitchen and the southwest corner of the laundry room in the northwest corner of the basement. The furnace and fuel room is long and narrow and takes up the rest of the north part of the basement.

Over the east half of the furnace room is the library, and west of it are two small bedrooms. Since our house was planned during the hot summer of 1934, windows are placed directly opposite each other with partition doors between to give each room the full benefit of all summer breezes.

Well, was that what you wanted to know?

(Later we constructed a cave under the ground along the west side of the north wall of the house. It is entered through the laundry room.)

TODAY'S article is devoted to answering questions asked by readers. Many of the inquiries are about the schoolboys. Apparently a good many readers have boys in or almost ready for high school and they are wondering about different things.

Yes, the boys wear overalls to school. One washday I suggested that one boy wear his light wash trousers so that I could wash his overalls. He hesitated a moment and said, "Well, Mother, I could wear them, but one day one of the other boys wore his good trousers and all the other kids made fun of him all day." So we compromised; he wore a pair of work trousers that couldn't be considered too sissified to wear to school.

The boys of this family wear blue bib overalls. Some of the others wear the striped ones, but our two eldest wore them when they were smaller and they feel the blue ones are more grown-up. Those with a belt instead of a bib are absolutely taboo because "all the little kids wear that kind." Oddly enough, when I am at the county seat I notice the boys there wear the blue belted trousers and no stripes or bibs are to be seen. No doubt each town has its own approved apparel.

Vaughn does part of his lessons at home, but so far Charles hasn't brought any books home to study. I cannot answer the question about grades yet, for they are just having the six weeks' tests. Maybe they wouldn't want me to tell after they hear. I know Vaughn isn't too optimistic.

Yes, they like school. It is quite embarrassing for them in one way, since having had only girls for schoolmates they know none of the games boys play. Since there is so much fieldwork and so many chores awaiting them at home each night and Saturday, they haven't had time to play at home. But they vow they are going to practice playing ball next summer. And they are trying to learn the rules. It is quite mortifying, when they are permitted to try their hand at playing, not to know what to do or when to do it.

Sadly enough there are more girls than boys in their classes. They really hadn't thought about girls being in high school at all. All the high school students of their acquaintance were boys. It was a terrible disappointment to them when one of the girls was elected class president. My guess is that they will feel more kindly toward them before finishing high school.

How big is the home town? I dislike to boast, but since you asked me I'll admit that there are supposed to be 397 people living there. That may be an exaggeration. I couldn't say. But if it is, it is in proportion to the population claims of similar metropolises. No, the boys do not go to Moravia to school. We live much closer to Blakesburg.

Perhaps I can answer the other questions some other time. But now I'd like to ask one myself. Are any of your schools as countrified as ours?

UNTIL recently I didn't realize that a good many Iowa boys read the farm page. The two in whom I am most interested read it. I had supposed they were checking up to see that I didn't tell too many things they didn't want told. Now I know there are boys all over the state checking up on what I say. I will have to be very careful that I do not slander boys in general.

Some of the younger boys wanted to know how big the boys in this family are. In answer to my question there was some difference of opinion about their weight. Vaughn thinks they each weighed seventy-two pounds the last time they were weighed. Charles thinks it was eighty-two. They wear age 14 overalls. They are almost exactly the same height. Just now we measured Charles. He is five feet one-fourth inch tall in his heelless house slippers.

They wear size 5 1/2 shoes. Charles has a cowlick, so he has to comb his hair straight back or part it on the right side if he happens to remember to comb it. His hair is a bit wavy. Vaughn has unruly, straight hair with a tinge of rust in it to match his freckles.

They despise going to bed. They hate to get up. (Are other eleven- and thirteen-year-olds about that size too?) I know people older than that who are about that size when it comes to retiring or arising.

The boys are anxious to get well enough so they can be outside to ride their new pony. They have seen her through the window and they think she is a dandy. She is bigger than Ted, their bay pony. He weighs seven hundred pounds. She is brown and weighs nine hundred pounds. Her name is Daisy, so now they wish they hadn't named Fawn's calf Daisy May.

Maybe you could tell more about their size if I told you they like to listen to the radio. So do I, but not all the time. They turn it down as low as possible to help lengthen the time that they will be allowed to listen before I issue the ultimatum that I have heard all the radio programs I can hear for one day.

They like to go to the attic and rummage. They bring all kinds of things downstairs for me to see, and they forget to take them back. Then I have to go to the attic and straighten up disordered trunks, boxes, and cupboards. (Are any of you about that size?)

They are likely to go off to school without their overshoes if I am not watching, forgetting that although a winter morning may be nice and sunny we may get rain or snow before nightfall.

They are quite willing to help with whatever work we are doing but often forget their regular daily chores until we remind them. Often they forget to close gates. They are good to take care of their little brothers but they are sure they never did all the things "those kids" find to do.

They will be starting to high school soon. I am glad they will have had chicken pox, scarlet fever, and whooping cough before they start to town school. I wish we didn't have to think about mumps and measles. Wouldn't it be nice if we could vaccinate for them?

WHITE SHOES likes cream. When the smallest boy turned her into the kitchen this morning she promptly emptied the pan of cream she found on the table. This pleased Bruce and the cat. The rest of us were not overjoyed. We had no cream for dinner and we shall have none for supper. There is plenty in the ten-gallon can, but it is sour and like White Shoes we prefer it sweet.

I have no love, admiration, or respect for cats. I admit I have no proof this world was not made for cats as well as for humans. I suppose they have a right to live here. They may be useful; I don't know. So long as they do not bother me I'm willing to tolerate them. They may have a poor opinion of me, but they do not hurt my feelings by letting me know it.

Cats resemble people. Some of them are wiser than others. Some of them are better behaved than others. There are Tabbies and Spots who are experts at catching mice and rats. Other felines excel only at sleeping in the sun. That is to be expected. All men are not good mechanics, nor are all women able to cook and sew. We are prone to judge others by our own likes and accomplishments.

We have not given White Shoes credit for being above average in intelligence. To us she has been an ordinary, lazy, stupid cat who enjoys sitting at the kitchen door waiting to be fed, but who will catch mice if she gets hungry enough. She doesn't have much time to loaf on the doorstep at present. She has four hungry kittens who get quite sarcastic when she lies down to rest instead of going back after another mouse for them.

Probably the cream gave her an idea. If the kittens were nearer the house the baby might feed them good things as he does their mother when he has the opportunity. If their persistent mewing disturbed the family as much as it did White Shoes perhaps everyone would hunt something for them to eat. Then she could catch up on her daydreaming and wouldn't have to spend all her time foraging. But White Shoes isn't the kind of cat who could find happiness carrying four heavy kittens, one at a time, from the woodpile to the house on a hot day. She may have told them of the cream and goodies to be found in the kitchen. If she did, it didn't do any good. Her babies were quite satisfied where they were.

So White Shoes caught another mouse, but when the children came to meet her she refused to give it to any of them. Head held high, she carried it across the barnyard followed by her wondering family. When their fears overcame them and they started back toward their safe woodpile, their mother stopped and waited. The fragrance of the tempting morsel she held brought them back. On came the procession, single file, through the yard, gate, and on to the house. The old cat knew better than to leave them at the back door. At the first unusual sound the youngsters would have scampered back to their former home. Instead she took them under the front porch where they could remain in hiding until they became bold enough to come out on exploring expeditions.

Is it a disgrace to be lazy? If White Shoes had been an enterprising cat she might not have stopped to think that her progeny were quite able to walk. She would have carried them in the time-honored custom of mother cats on moving day. Her indolence caused her to use her brain to save her muscles. We praise the labor-saving devices in our homes, in factories, and on our farms. But if it were not for the slothful ones who dream of ways to avoid dull toil we would have few inventions.

The idlers we despise may be thinking diligently as we are laboring. Who are we to say which is stupid, the dreamer or the over zealous toiler?

I N S P I R E D by the reading of *Swiss Family Robinson,* the younger members of the family have selected names for various places on this farm.

The elevation upon which most of our farm buildings and the dwelling stand has been called Pine Tree Hill by Vaughn ever since we came here. Before the road was graveled, the hill was called any number of names by travelers who became stuck in the clay when they tried to motor up the grade. None of the names I heard were very complimentary, so I prefer Pine Tree Hill.

Irvin suggested that the big hill over by the spring be called Spring Hill. His brothers argued that there were two hills there. The matter was settled by naming them North Spring Hill and South Spring Hill. Steep Hill is the only way to describe the hill between here and the spring, but there is talk of calling it Orchard Hill since there was an orchard there until the dry summer of 1936.

The thirty-eight acres of woodland north of the spring is named Oursylvania. Two good reasons for this, I am told, are that it is our timberland and Grandma Faber was born in Pennsylvania.

West of the farmstead we find Buckbrush Hill; if we cross

Green Valley and skirt around Mosquito Bayou we come to the creek. The boys are sorry they cannot name the stream because it is already called Soap Creek. They insist it isn't quite fair for every branch of Big Soap, North Soap, South Soap, or Little Soap to be called Soap Creek. Our creek is one of the sources of North Soap; thus it would be heresy to call it anything but Soap Creek.

On the other side of the creek stands Gooseberry Hill; it could have been called Walnut Hill but since there are walnut trees everywhere the appellation was saved for one of the valleys not yet named. At present the matter under discussion is whether to call the largest valley in Oursylvania Hot Valley, Dogwood Valley, or Rabbit Hollow.

Now that I was back in Monroe County and writing for more newspapers, more people wrote to ask questions about the family. Some of the inquiries came from new readers of the *Tribune* and the *Iowegian*. To answer them I wrote the following column.

WE are a very ordinary farm family. Although we have four sons and no daughters at all even that is not unusual. Quite frequently we learn of other families consisting of a father, a mother, and four sons.

Perhaps we have more books than many farm families. One of my earliest ambitions was to own hundreds of books. Everybody, including Santa Claus, helped me to realize that ambition by giving me books instead of other gifts. I liked toys and games but I could play with those belonging to my sister and brothers, while I could treasure the books for my very own. When I grew older I acquired the habit of buying books instead of hats, furniture, or curtains. Although I wanted the garments and house furnishings I saw in the show windows at the county seat, I couldn't buy them and the books, too. Thus we have more books but we are a bit shabbier and our furniture is a bit more ancient and more badly scarred than found in the average farm home. Otherwise we have no claim to distinction.

With Skippy, the dog of many breeds; Tom, Lady Grey, and the four cat children; the usual assortment of speckled hens, baaing sheep, fat lazy hogs, black and red cows; a lone Jersey; Ted, the bay pony; Roger and Barney, the old work team; Brooke, the three-year-old filly; our dilapidated furniture; and our ton of books we live on a 240-acre farm in southeastern Iowa. The two big boys ride their bicycles or drive our 1930 Model A sedan five miles to the high school in the nearest village, a metropolis of 443 inhabitants. Over the clay hills to the south of us the two little boys trudge until they reach the white, one-room schoolhouse that stands on top of the highest hill.

Our greatest ambitions are to own a tractor and an electric lighting plant that generates electricity by wind power. Nearly all the other neighbors have tractors that travel faster than Old Roger and Barney. Many of the neighbors have electricity. They have radios and gasoline washers. If we get the light plant, we'll buy a radio and an electric washer, too.

One of our chief sources of pride is living in a house built by our own hands. It isn't quite finished and it isn't a model of perfection, but we are proud of it. Over five years ago we began building. We moved into the basement when we had half of two rooms floored and half the shingles on the roof. Gradually we made it livable, then comfortable. Spare time is something of which the farmer talks very often. Until he attempts to build a house during the slack seasons he doesn't understand what a scarce commodity spare time is on a farm. However, one can do what one wants very much to do if only one has the patience and determination.

Our furnace was installed one rainy day. Just before corn-picking one fall we put up the siding over the sheathing. The following autumn we put in the water system. Baseboards and casings were planed and put in place and the bookshelves in the library were built on stormy winter days. We are proud of our interior woodwork, which is from walnut grown here on the farm and largely hand-planed.

We are not so proud of pencil marks, crayon drawings, and various other blemishes created by the two younger sons before they were old enough to go to school. Apparently most people have some possessions in which they may take pride and others that they hope nobody will notice.

Likewise all children make their parents proud of them at some times and utterly ashamed at others. Like all children our sons contrive to make us happy or ashamed when we least expect it. Yes, we are a very ordinary farm family.

IT was Sunday morning. Because it would soon be time to get
ready for Sunday school the two younger members of the
family were hurrying to get their playing done before they had
to come inside and take their baths. They were not outside during all of their playing. There was much running in and out—
hurrying back into the basement rooms after treasures and hurrying out without taking time for the unimportant task of closing
the doors to keep the warm air out-of-doors.

"Bang! Bang!" sounded what is left of our back porch screen
as it swung back and forth on the one hinge that remains unbroken. Bang! Bang! There isn't much rest, not even on Sunday—
especially not on Sunday—for screen doors in the home of a few
boys.

"Mother, what can I feed Lady Grey? She's hungry."

"Get some dry bread out of the green crock on the worktable."

"We fed that to her."

"There are some meat scraps."

"She ate them, Mother."

"Then those cold biscuits."

"We fed them to Tom and the kittens."

"Look at me," comes a call from the outside, and the grey
lady's caretaker rushes to see what wonders are being performed
in the box elder trees that stand beside the back door.

All is quiet for a time. Then excited voices call me to the
back porch where there is a cluster of excited boys and one
uncle—an excited uncle it was, too—around Mac's cage.

"Lady Grey was after Mac, Mother. She jumped up on the
wall and knocked the plate off the milk and got some of Mac's
feathers in the milk, Mother. She was trying to eat him. Would
she eat Mac, Mother?"

"The door wasn't clear shut. Somebody didn't shut the door.
It was open a little way at the bottom, Mother. She came right
in on the porch. Do you suppose Mac will die, Mother?"

"I hope not. I don't think he is hurt very much, just frightened. Now keep the door closed; shut it carefully every time you
go outside, or she will eat him next time."

"Oh, we will, Mother. We don't want her to eat Mac."

And they did shut it—the next four or five times they ran
in or out.

O N the front porch sat the birdcage, silent and empty. Flying as beautifully as if he had lived out there all his life, Mac the canary soared to the top of the big pine tree.

"Can we catch him, Mother? I didn't know he'd get out, Mother, honest I didn't. Could I climb up and get him?"

"Chee?" asked Mac, looking down at us.

"He'd just fly away. You know how hard he is to catch when he gets loose in the house. Why did you bring him out here? I thought you were going to take him to the back porch."

"You didn't tell me. I didn't know he'd get out. Can he live out here, Mother? Or will it be too cold for him when winter comes?"

"He will be gone before winter. He will be lucky if he lives a day or two. A cat, hawk, owl, or anything could catch him. He wouldn't know how to get away. Besides he would starve to death. He wouldn't know how to find anything to eat."

"Chee," reproached Mac, pecking at the limb on which he sat.

"I'll put some feed in the cage and leave the door open, Mother. Maybe he will come down here when he gets hungry."

The object of our worry flew down to a huge branch three or four feet above my head. A belligerent sparrow hopped down beside him. There was just a chance that a good thrashing might send him down to us for safety. But the sparrow flew away. He had lost interest in a silly canary that would not even look at him. Mac puffed out his throat and trilled forth the loveliest aria of all those he has composed and sung for us during the four years he has been one of the family.

An hour passed. Mac seemed quite content in the pine tree.

Field workers have to eat, so I went to the kitchen. If Mac would stay another hour until the boss and the eldest came in for the noon meal the entire family might be able to catch him. Noon came. There was no canary singing in the pine tree. He was not in any of the other trees in the yard, chicken lot, or hog pasture.

Presently he was seen in the grass near the garden gate. We surrounded him. He slipped away, just how we don't know, and flew up into one of the cedar trees. Vaughn climbed. Mac flew higher. Vaughn ascended the other branch and reached out for the ball of yellow feathers.

Mac flew to the picket fence. Now we had him. From outside Vaughn reached through between the pickets while we guarded this side. The runaway crept between the post and a picket. He flew to another cedar tree. Being followed there, he flew to the tall maple in the garden. When his pursuer climbed out upon one branch, Mac flew to another and then another. Each time he waited until he felt the touch of the boy's hand before he slipped away.

The third time he waited too long. It was rather difficult to climb down to the fork of the tree with the trembling songster in one hand. Once there the boy reached down. I reached up, and Mac was in my hand. Back in the cage, the bird didn't present his usual gay appearance. His feathers were rumpled. There was green grass stain on his beak. He looked tired and shaky. But he wasn't ready to admit that.

"Chee," he scolded, peering into his empty water dish. The drink was brought to him immediately.

THIS largest egg is a bad one," remarked Charles, as he entered the kitchen with the day's gathering of eggs.

"Why do you think it is bad? It appears perfectly fresh to me," I protested.

"I know it is a bad egg, because I found it in The Jail," retorted my son with a grin.

It does seem as though a woman who had been accustomed to brothers before she acquired a husband and sons wouldn't grab the bait every time, but some of us do. I don't mind it at all and it helps amuse the men—especially if they themselves have fallen for the same gag earlier in the day.

Perhaps I ought to make some explanation about The Jail. This edifice is very useful when our sons have company. It makes a lovely place, so I am told, for whoever has the honor of being sheriff to put his prisoners.

The eldest and his three assistants wasted a great deal of perspiration constructing this building. It was made from the body of a car someone had discarded. The roof was made from odds and ends of boards, tin, and whatever could be confiscated for the purpose without too much objection from the boss. (A man with four sons is very lucky if he can keep any nails, boards, or anything else for his own. Having learned this, Dick waits as silently as human nature will permit for the lads to grow up, at which time he imagines they will cease to bother his tools, nails, and lumber. He may learn differently then.) The Jail was built. Luckily for my peace of mind, the structure is behind the barn where it doesn't show too much from the road. I just cannot believe it improves the appearance of our farmstead, but then I have queer notions.

The beautiful thing, the handy thing, about this jailhouse is that the car door—there was only one door—makes a very lovely door for The Jail. Vaughn invented a lock of some sort by which he can secure this "front" door to ensure the keeping of the prisoners. Please do not ask me to explain the mechanism of the lock. Although I know nothing about machinery, I think a two by four is part of it. I couldn't be positive about that, though. The two by four may have some other purpose I'm not wise enough to understand.

If any of my youthful readers know where there is a junk pile that has the body of an ancient motorcar upon it, and if their parents are not too unreasonable about the appearance of their barnyard or chicken lot; I'd advise them to secure that car body at once if they are in need of a prison. Otherwise some other boys might get there first.

Of course, a few fingers might be smashed as the door swings shut. And sometimes the sheriff may forget about the inmates and leave them shut within its torrid interior some hot day when the sun is directly overhead. But boys are accustomed to minor discomfort. When it is play instead of work that brings discomfort, boys don't mind it at all.

On a farm where there are boys a jail is a near necessity. It doesn't seem quite fair that there might be jailless boys on other farms or in cities when we have The Jail in all its hideous glory to keep us happy.

ONE reader writes that the article about Effie May was the most interesting one I have written recently. Another writes that her family enjoys reading about Effie May.

Reading about Effie May may be all right, but this family doesn't enjoy hearing about her. Any news about that calf is bad news, always. Just last week there came a sprinkle on washday. The sun came out later, but the socks didn't get quite dry by the time the other garments were brought into the house. There didn't seem to be any reason why they shouldn't be left on the clothesline overnight. The next day I found half of them on the grass under the clothesline.

Effie May was in the brooder house eating the chickens' shelled corn as innocently as a pup eating his first egg. Nobody had driven her out of there since the evening before. How was she to know she wasn't supposed to be in there that day?

She was quite uninterested when I asked her if she was the

one who had chewed and ruined one of each pair of the big boys' best school socks. Just by looking at her anyone could tell that she wouldn't have thought of doing such a thing. However, the line is so high that I have to reach up to fasten or unfasten the clothespins. And I am five feet five and one-half inches tall. The lambs out there in the chicken lot might have enjoyed nibbling at the hosiery, but Effie May would have had to yank it down for them first. For so small a calf it must have taken some tiptoeing. Since her time is not very valuable, it didn't matter if it did take quite a while.

Being very small for her age hasn't seemed to be much of a handicap to Effie May. Persistence and patience have succeeded in making her life one grand exhilarating adventure after another for the four months of her existence. There is a possibility that she may have attempted stunts that she didn't manage to accomplish. To one who has become quite well acquainted with her during those four months, it doesn't seem possible. Effie May couldn't have wasted much time at things she didn't get done. She has accomplished too much in her short life for one to believe she has met many failures.

All summer we have pondered the question. Why is there a calf such as Effie May? And since she exists, why does she belong to us? Why couldn't somebody who likes michievous calves own her, so we could have had a more sedate and heavier built calf in her stead?

But now I understand why she belongs to us. If I had known sooner that her purpose in life was to entertain *Tribune* readers, many more pages about Effie May might have been written. It is a great relief to know that they find her amusing. We don't.

T H E melting snow left our roads very muddy, so I was not surprised that Bruce, our youngest schoolboy, was late getting home. At 5 P.M. when he was still not here I was sure he was having trouble on the clay hills. The boss came from the field with his load of corn, and I told him I was going to meet the missing boy. He suggested that we look first to see if the big boys were in sight. If they should happen to get a ride part of the way they might be home early enough that Vaughn could ride Ted over the hills to meet the tardy one. No boys could be seen along the road or down the railroad tracks, but Dick thought he caught a glimpse of Bruce coming up one of the hills. So I went over to the sheep shed to look for eggs.

When I returned no boys had come yet, so I started down the hill toward the mailbox in the gathering darkness. Before I reached the corner where the gravel turns to the west and the clay hills lead south to the schoolhouse I met Bruce. His coat was unbuttoned. Plastered with mud from head to foot, he was a sorry sight. One high topped overshoe was half off and dragged along in the mud as he walked. On the other foot was a muddy (that is an inadequate description but muddy will have to do) stocking, the lower half of which was about halfway up in what was supposed to be the stocking leg.

"I got stuck over by the schoolhouse," he announced, "but I couldn't make the teacher hear me. I lost one overshoe, and here is my shoe. I couldn't get it back on my foot," he ended as he handed me a large lump of mud. It didn't look like a shoe to me, but I broke off some of the cold mud and found a bit of leather.

Our progress back up the hill to the house was somewhat slow. We had to walk off the gravel in the mud because of the stockinged foot. I couldn't get the overshoe back on the lad's foot because his shoe inside it also had slipped partly off. (If you are confused trying to follow my fractured syntax, think how confused I was out there in all that mud. I'm not going to try to rewrite that sentence. Please try to figure out for yourself what I mean.)

So—I heard the story of the adventure from the boy as he clung to my hand, hopping and limping along. Sometimes he hummed cheerfully out of sheer delight at seeing one of his family again. At other times he was filled with self-pity for what he had endured. It seems that he hadn't thought anyone would come to hunt for him. While he was stuck in the mud, he expected to be there forever. He was surprised to learn that the other boys were not home from high school and that we hadn't eaten supper yet.

"I just wished if it hadn't been for school," he said. (Can you translate that? I did.) "I think I'll stay home now until spring comes. When it gets warm, I'll start to school again. I'm through my first reader."

Once again there are only two schoolboys in our family. The two youngest are having a happy time doing all the things they used to do before Bruce started to school. School is wonderful, but home can be a pretty nice place, too.

As for myself, I'm quite satisfied. I'd be glad if we could get Bruce to stay home until March brings spring thaws. Then maybe he would be content to be a first grader until fall. Seven is young enough to enter second grade. Even though he might make only one grade a year, he could reach high school before he became decrepit.

D O W N at the barn much bleating is to be heard. Some of the mother ewes have lost their fleeces, while their children are shut in the barn with the other ewes that haven't been sheared yet. Other baby sheep—good-sized for baby sheep but yet babies as long as they are the youngest, like human babies— are baaing quite plaintively because their mothers are within the barn and they have escaped outside with the wrong bunch of sheep.

Charles thinks the task of feeding extra hands is as much work as that of the sheepshearers. He doesn't have very good fuel and he has had trouble with his baking today. One of the loaves of bread refused to get brown and two others were burned. His cake fell, and the potatoes will not boil. All his kindling was burned when he ran short of wood, and last night's shower has dampened both the kindling and the new load of wood that was brought to him. He feels just as many another cook has felt on similar occasions.

Each of the boys had to have the fleece from his sheep weighed as soon as it was clipped. To date Vaughn can boast that one of his sheep had the heaviest wool, but Irvin has two ewes yet to be sheared and Charles has one who is wearing her winter coat in spite of the summer temperatures.

Just now the cook left to inquire how the shearing is progressing. He is very anxious to know how much wool money he will have to spend. As soon as he went out the door I heard the ham in the skillet frying merrily. Perhaps the potatoes will boil, too, if he doesn't watch them too closely.

When I went into the kitchen to see how things were progressing, I felt a bit discouraged myself. A skillet in which eggs had been fried was sitting on top of the warming oven, and in it was one of my best tablespoons. I knew just how Charles felt about his troubles, but I'm sure he didn't know how I felt about the tablespoon of that set having been used on the hot stove and discolored with eggs.

That, remarked the cook, was what Dad did when he came in and fried some eggs at noon. He was pretty much relieved to think that he hadn't been the one who did it. When I suggested that the good spoons be returned to the dining room where they belong and the matter not be mentioned to the boss who has plenty of troubles of his own, Charles agreed with me. Hereafter, I think he will watch his assistants to see that they take proper care of the silverware.

Sheepshearing is hard work, I've heard. But I'm not sure who is working the hardest: sheepshearers, the two small boys who are watching, the cook, or the cook's mother, who finds it impossible to stay out of the kitchen and offer advice to the sweating worker there.

T HE younger members of the family are quite sad. It was cold last night, so Little Sister, the grey kitten, slept with the cows to keep warm. This morning the boys found her smashed flat on the concrete floor.

"Sugar was the one who killed her," they explained, "but she hadn't known the kitty was there, so we can't blame her for it. Little Sister ought to have known better."

However, she hadn't, and there is one less cat to howl at the back door when they see a plate of table scraps coming. Little Sister caught a good many mice during her short career. I guess she paid us well for the trouble she caused. I regret her going, if only for the sorrow it caused her four young masters.

Felix and the black cat ought to be able to catch all the mice in the barn and granary. And two cats are still two too many to please me.

To be quite honest, I don't believe I hate cats as much as I say. They are hateful creatures when they get into the milk bucket. They are most aggravating underfoot when one is carrying a load of wood or two buckets of milk or water. No matter how much a child loves a cat, a germ-conscious mother doesn't like to see the two together.

I like to see kittens playing or a mother cat stalking a mouse in the granary or sitting on a fence post washing her face. But cats, like our children and our neighbors, are most interested in their own happiness. They are not greatly concerned about what we want them to do. If they can suit us while suiting themselves, they enjoy our approval. But they are not going to a lot of bother if our wishes do not coincide with theirs. Much as I hate to find a purring pussy lapping up the cream off a pail of milk on the milk shelf, I can't make her feel guilty about it.

Felines are like humans in one respect; they love to be praised and petted. But they are not going to correct any of their faults in order to be better liked. They know that people despise them for their failings; they hate to be scolded but they go right ahead and do things they know hadn't ought to be done, hoping they'll not get caught and hoping they'll be forgiven if they are.

I guess that is why children think so much of cats. They haven't yet learned to excuse only their own faults and condemn those of all other living creatures.

PERHAPS you are not interested in hearing about the strange disappearance of Felix. I can't keep from writing about it, for I'm worried. I've been searching for him ever since he vanished. I have no love for Felix nor any other cat. You may think it queer that I am spending so much time wondering where he is and looking in impossible places for His Catship.

The last time I saw him he was going upstairs in the arms of the youngest member of the family. Kitty's young master is not in the habit of casting his pet out into the uncertainties of the weather unless he is forced or cajoled into it. Possibly Felix was thrust out-of-doors by some member of the family who has forgotten about it. (By this time all of them know that Mother doesn't approve of cats in the house.) Maybe he has gone to live with some of the neighbors who will have a deeper appreciation of his worth. I hope so. But I fear he hasn't.

I've opened closet doors, trunk lids, and dresser drawers. I've peered into cupboards, boxes, and baskets. I've looked under some of the loose boards in the attic floor. Knowing that a certain youngster likes to put a cushion on the sleeping feline and then fall upon it, giggling while Felix squirms out, I have moved every pillow and cushion half expecting to find the lifeless body of the wretched little creature.

At my busiest moments I imagine I hear pathetic mews. I hurry down or upstairs and start the search all over again. At last, convinced that no spot remains where a cat could be concealed, I go back to my duties. I think of another likely location where a lad might jail an offender and again ascend or descend the stairs.

While writing this I've remembered that I didn't look under that unused featherbed or beneath any of the mattresses. I can see about that tonight. But there's the attic floor. I didn't raise half the boards. I wish we had taken time to nail them down. Anyway, it is too big a task to attempt tonight. I'll have to put it off until tomorrow.

A member of the *Tribune* family writes that our loss of Felix, the cat, in a cream can was not so expensive as her loss; she found an old ten-gallon milk can filled with chickens nearly large enough to fry. She discovered the chickens the day after her small son had shut them up in the can.

I'll admit that Felix wasn't much of a loss to me, since I do not admire cats—and we have seven others. But the lad who canned the poultry didn't choose a can that was in use, so his mother didn't have to rinse, wash, scald, and air the can and then wash, rinse, scald, and air it again as I did this one. I have a queer sort of feeling about it yet. I don't put cream in it unless all the others are filled. Yet, although I wouldn't like the task, I'd prefer to clean up a can—a can that looked perfectly clean in the first place—yes, I'd be willing to go through all that *again* rather than give up ten gallons of young fries.

We've had chickens commit suicide by hanging or drowning themselves. They've been eaten by swine, cats, and various varmints. They've been choked to death by admiring small boys. Some froze to death and others died from the summer heat. One died from fright when I unintentionally scared her off the nest. Once my dad and I were catching old roosters to take to market, and we had to run one of them down to catch him. When we picked him up he ceased to breathe, and we didn't take him to town. We've found hens who had starved to death under buckets and boxes. But as yet we haven't lost a chicken in a cream can.

One of our young pullets cut her throat by eating a sharp piece of glass. One spring a playful puppy carried the corpses of the game it had killed into the poultry yard, and I had the pleasure of burying twenty-nine nice fat capons one morning because they had eaten some of the decayed flesh. A pet lamb chewed several baby chicks to death one spring. Once four chicks met death when I upset a can of kerosene upon them.

Possibly there are other methods by which fowls can end their careers and surprise their owners. If so our chickens just haven't discovered them yet, but I'm sure they have done their best to invent new ways of dying.

R E C E N T L Y we had a real Iowa-style summer storm— complete with thunder, lightning, wind, rain, and hail. The morning after the rain the sun was bright and beautiful. Of course, the hay would be slower in curing. But we didn't mind since the garden, the new alfalfa, the oats, the corn, and the second crop of clover and alfalfa benefited.

Perhaps the chinch bugs would be hindered still further; there might be an oat crop to harvest yet. On this farm the hail had done no damage, although the heavy cloud had come near enough to fling marble-sized chuncks of ice at us for a few moments.

After the excessive heat that preceded the storm, the fresh air was very welcome. However Mac, the canary, was restless and did more chirping than singing. For some time I pretended to misunderstand his pleadings. The back porch isn't altogether safe for trustful birds who know little of danger. But he insisted and sang his clearest, loudest notes of thankfulness when I carried him out there into the fresh air.

Some time later two serious boys stood with me and stared at the overturned, empty cage on the porch floor, at the gaping hole where the screen had been torn loose from the door, and at the pitifully small remnant of feathers on the floor of the implement shed.

Lady Grey and her four children—Spot, Ring, Dirty Face, and Rover—stopped washing their faces and looked at us hopefully but nobody thought of bringing them anything to eat.

"Why did you do it?" we asked. But the grey lady only rounded her back and purred happily thinking that we were making a call upon her family.

Someone said the two small boys petted the cats so much that they stayed around the house. The boss wishes we had put the cage in an upstairs window instead of on the porch. I have wished a good many things that it is too late to do. Charles remarked that it was two years ago this week since Mac escaped from his cage and spent a happy morning in the treetops before we captured him. The two little boys said nothing intelligible, but their tears spoke eloquently. Neither has asked for anything to feed the cats lately.

Somehow I have not wanted to carry the empty cage to the attic although I cleaned it and set it back upon the porch shelf. Nor have I asked one of the boys to take it.

That tiny, feathered morsel of happiness that found cage life such a joyous existence for seven short years is going to be missed in this family. The empty cage, the rumpled feathers in a bottle in the curio cabinet, and the memory of that strong, silvery voice are all that we have left of the bit of our hearts that was Mac, the canary.

SUNDAY mornings are nice. It gives one a deliciously lazy feeling to lie abed until 5:30 or 6 A.M., even knowing it will be necessary to hurry after arising in order to get the chores done in time to go to Sunday school.

Presently the insistent demands of the outraged stock, who do not like the idea of such a late breakfast, can be ignored no longer. With another yawn and a few groans, which might be classified as unhappy groans because the night could not be extended longer or contented groans because this was one morning the alarm didn't awaken everybody before they were through sleeping, the farm family arises.

It is pleasant to see the house in its Sunday morning neatness, fresh from its Saturday cleaning and dusting. All will not be so spic-and-span ere nightfall, so the farm housewife gloats over its unusual perfection while she may.

The morning meal is even more substantial than the usual weekday farm breakfast. Everybody is hungry because it is late, and it is a good plan to eat heartily because the noon meal is almost sure to be late. The family does eat heartily, but the cook and housewife is apt to think of the many things that have to be done before 10:00 A.M. and jump up from the table after a few half-hearted nibbles at whatever eatables happen to be nearest her plate.

After the dishwashing and bedmaking comes the sweeping. While Charles is peeling the potatoes and slicing the meat for dinner, one of the younger members of the family does the dusting more or less efficiently and thoroughly. There is only a thin coat of dust for there isn't so much dirt to sweep out on Sunday morning. Somebody turned one of the lamps too high the previous evening and the chimney is smoked but there isn't time to clean it now.

All those in the house must hurry to finish their baths and scramble into clean clothing before those outside come in from their chores and need a few errand runners to bring shoes, socks, ties, or whatever these last-minute dressers may need. Always there is a missing button to be sewn or a mislaid garment to be found, even though the housekeeper was sure everything was in order for once.

We reviewed the Sunday school lesson together in order that those who haven't studied it can answer any questions that are asked.

There is a peep into the cupboards and refrigerator to be sure the salad is setting and there is enough cake and pie in case visitors are brought back to share the noon meal; there is a hurried trip to be sure that the poultry have plenty of water in case the family goes home with some other family to spend the day.

Those already in the car shout, "Hurry up!" The late ones turn on the night lock, making sure that they have taken the key along, and start to the car. Somebody sees that a pig, calf, or lamb is out and all hands rush to put it back in its proper place.

Meanwhile, all the neighbors' cars have passed. The chase after the truant of the livestock has made shoes dusty and given the whole family a disheveled appearance. There is a bit of argument over who gets to drive and who has to ride in the back seat, and once more the miracle of getting off to Sunday school not very, if at all, late has been accomplished.

During the late 1930s I started corresponding with several of my *Tribune* readers. Not only did we exchange personal letters but I included excerpts from many of their letters in my columns. My readers became familiar not only with me and my family but also many other readers through these columns. A desire grew for us to meet in person. A picnic was arranged in August 1941, and we have met annually ever since—for almost forty years now. My instructor in one of the courses I took at the Elderhostel at the University of Iowa in the summer of 1980 had attended the first picnic as a small child. Following is the newspaper account of that first gathering of my readers.

NEARLY 100 AT PICNIC WITH 'FARM WOMAN'
By J. S. Russell
The Tribune's Farm Editor

INDIANOLA, IA—Nearly 100 persons, mostly from southern Iowa, met at Lake Ahquabi state park near here Sunday on a 'blind date' picnic.

They had one thing in common: they had read Elizabeth Beresford's "A Farm Woman Speaks Up" in The Tribune farm page.

With a very few exceptions, none of the folks attending the picnic ever had seen Elizabeth Beresford and few even knew that her real name is Mrs. Inez Faber. She lives near Moravia, Ia.

Many of the women present Sunday had written letters to Elizabeth and some of these letters had been published in the column.

And so Mrs. Faber had a great time visiting with "Sandra" and "Iva" and "The Poor Farm Woman" as they put their picnic dinners together and exchanged notes about their farm homes and their families.

They all knew of Mrs. Faber and her family and many of them knew of each other, but none were acquainted personally until Sunday.

Mrs. Faber introduced her husband, R. A. Faber, and her four sons Charles, Vaughn, Bruce and Irvin, as she shed the anonymity that she had assumed as Elizabeth Beresford during more than ten years.

Especially did "The Farm Woman" enjoy, she said, visiting with Mrs. Mari Josephine Niendorf of Van Meter; Mrs. Alice Lawless of Truro; Mrs. H. A. Stewart of Dexter; Mrs. Florence Dattillo of Derby and a number of others who had written to her during the years since she started the column.

The women wanted to know which of the Faber boys had been sick and which one was kicked in the face by the pony and Mrs. Faber was kept busy posing for snapshots so that everyone would have something by which to remember the day.

Without any special invitations and without much advance notice, farm folks came from a dozen counties to attend the first Tribune Farm Page picnic and to meet Elizabeth.

Nearly 90 persons were registered and probably a few were there who forgot to register. Represented were Warren, Monroe, Clarke, Decatur, Madison, Poweshiek, Dallas, Polk, Jasper, Hamilton, Lucas and Marion counties.

From perhaps the greatest distance came the Peter Peterson family, from near Webster City, and the six in the family equaled the record of the Fabers. The Petersons drove 86 miles on a hot August day but Mrs. Peterson said it was worth it.

"How often have I read Elizabeth's comments and thought how like her own experiences mine had been," she said.

The picnic was mostly for the farm women, but the husbands came along, too, and several of the women said the men enjoyed "A Farm Woman Speaks Up" just as much as the homemakers.

9
The End of the 1930s

Vaughn and Charles attended Blakesburg High
School from the fall of 1938 to the spring of 1942. Both of Dick's
parents died in the spring of 1939 and my mother had an operation
for cancer in January of 1940.

Vaughn was thirteen and Charles only eleven when their high
school days started.

IT wasn't easy for an eleven-year-old and a thirteen-year-old
to do their chores and make the five-mile trip in bad weather
when they had to walk down the railroad track. During good
weather they rode their bicycles. When it was too cold for cycling,
they drove the car until the roads became snow blocked. Yes, at
the age of thirteen Vaughn regularly drove the car to school.

One stormy morning they came home quite exhausted from
walking through the deep snow. Not enough pupils had come for
classes to be held, and they had been sent home without having
had time to rest or to thaw their frosted feet. To this day Charles
maintains he has never been so cold as he was at that time. The
next morning I phoned to see if school would be in session.

"It depends on how many come. I can't tell you until I know
if there are going to be enough here to have school," I was told.

"I don't like for the boys to wade five miles through this deep
snow unless they will have school," I retorted.

"Oh, don't send them. It is too far for them to walk. I will
let you know." I am not sure how he thought they had been
getting to school since the snow came. Maybe he didn't realize
that our roads were blocked. Soon there was a call that there
would be classes that day.

It was a long, cold winter that year of 1939–1940. Henry

Horn, who lived down where the Hummaconna post office used to be, would watch them walking down the railroad track. He said it was the only time he ever saw children going to school as dawn was breaking.

The sounds and voices from downstairs indicated that the two older sons were getting ready for school. Although I couldn't understand what was said a great deal could be guessed about how things were progressing by the tones of each of the familiar voices.

Presently, I heard the second son talking over the telephone in the stair landing. At once the two youngest came upstairs to me. Never yet, when they have been in the house, has anyone found it possible to use the telephone without both of them going upstairs or downstairs during the conversation. Even though it was somewhat annoying to Charles who isn't very skilled at telephone talking, I was glad to have an opportunity to talk to his two younger brothers after they had slowly stumped their way up the stairs and drowned out all conversation.

"We are going to take the car. Tell him to be out to the road at eight o'clock," I heard Charles say. Just then the two youngest came into my room, the elder sniffing quite audibly; Vaughn had thumped him or administered some other form of brotherly punishment because he had bothered Charles. At my suggestion that they get washed and combed for school they disappeared.

Presently I heard the car leave. All was very quiet downstairs. Evidently the boss and Charles had finished the breakfast dishes before the boys left and the boss was busy at chores outdoors.

When I called to the two who were in the house the youngest came upstairs again. His next older brother yelled back that he had washed and combed. "Are you going to wash yourself, or do you want Bruce to do it?" I inquired. One must use diplomacy with the youngest.

"What?"

Frowningly concentrating on the important question while I repeated what he had heard the first time, the youngest came to a vital decision. "I want you to wash me."

"Very well. Bring me the washcloth."

Presently a very cold, dripping washcloth was brought to my bedside. With it I scoured most of the dirt from his face and some of it from his hands. He hurried down the stairs to the towel. In a few moments he was back with his overshoes to be fastened.

Then I heard a mad scramble as the search was on for coats, scarfs, caps, and mittens. From outside, their father came to give his assistance.

Once more the four sons had departed for another day at school. This is quite an event any day; and with the mother of the family being ill with the flu, it is quite a triumph to know that the big boys did manage to get started by eight and the little ones by eight-thirty.

W HEN I was a child our house was sheltered by huge maples and towering elms. An ancient oak at the east side of the house was an ideal spot for a swing. Just north of it, the tall lilac bushes kept the cool north winds away. And over the picket fence "the old garden" was full of blackberry vines and cherry, peach, and pear trees. Sometimes there was a swing under the big crab apple tree at the east end of this plot, which had been my grandmother's garden before it was given over to fruit and a new location fenced for the cultivation of strawberries and vegetables.

Of course, all our playing wasn't done at the east end of the house. There was a sandpile under the maples in the northwest corner of the yard. And by climbing the steps over the west yard fence we could get into the woodlot that was full of maples, also. Or if we chose to play on the wide stretches of bluegrass outside of the picket fence along the roadside or across the road by the rail fence there, we found plenty of shade, for two long rows of maples began on the other side of our barn—almost up at the Red Bridge—and reached to the schoolhouse on the corner.

Sometimes visitors symphathized with us because so many trees made the place seem so lonely, they said. We had never been lonesome.

My next home was back in the field, for there were thirty acres of pasture between the dwelling house and the road. It had been my other grandpa's home since he was two years old. Always it had been an entrancing place to me: the barn with its mysterious basement with the stalls; the smokehouse with a front porch and a loft full of interesting things; the wood house; the house itself with an outside entrance to the basement and also one from within the exciting pantry; the parlor with its strange furniture that appeared so new and shiny, yet was so different from that in the homes of younger people; the curio cabinet; the enlarged portraits of the grandmother and aunt who died long ago; and most thrilling of all the upstairs with its treasure of papers and magazines. People didn't see how I could bear to live there so far from everywhere. But I loved it, old furniture, ramshackle barn, and all.

When we moved to the farm we bought, some felt sorry for me because the kitchen was so small and some didn't see how I could bear to live on the flat upland. It was so monotonous, they said, with no hills or hollows but a never ending plain. But I liked small kitchens. I liked being able to see to the far corners of the farm. I even liked skimping and saving to make a payment on the mortgage each first of May.

Five years ago we moved again. "How can you bear it?" they ask. "With all those awful hills and hollows and trees to hide your livestock so you can't find them it must be an unhandy place to live. And isn't it terrible to be so far from town after you used to live so close? And the wind—why did you build on this dreadful hilltop?"

But we like it! It is home, as were the other three. It would be a queer family who didn't like home, who couldn't find some things about every farm that more than compensate for the few things that are not so pleasant.

THE youngest is dividing his time between the field where his dad is cultivating corn and the field where his big brother is giving the soybeans their weekly harrowing. Charles, my chief assistant, is working in the garden. These rains that are making the crops grow so rapidly are producing a bountiful crop of weeds.

The captain of the hoe has more than he can manage. When he gets the strawberries clean, the yard and poultry lot are full of weeds. The ragweeds and wild lettuce are choking the raspberries and the potatoes have begun to need attention. Before he knows it the strawberry vines are hidden again.

He doesn't have much time to spend compiling statistics pertaining to geography, sports, or almost anything else as he is so fond of doing. He did tell me yesterday that Iowa and Missouri have thirty-two counties with the same names. He also told me the number of counties in the United States but I have forgotten the exact number. He started to count the Iowa counties from which I had received letters from *Tribune* readers during 1933. But he didn't get through with that. He is anxious to count the number of cities in the United States. But if he is going to annihilate all these weeds so he can go on a camping trip next week he'd better postpone his city counting.

This afternoon he has a helper. Part of the time the helper is on the back porch playing with the bee smoker. Again he examines the flies, bugs, and moths caught on the fly ribbon or gets the *Tribune* and hints that nobody has read Popeye to him yet today. He is supposed to be pulling the weeds around the back porch. He takes spurts of working industriously at the task. Some of the flowers may give up their lives but it is for a good cause. They couldn't live if the weeds were not pulled. At present the weeds are flying again. Their five-year-old enemy works when he does work, which isn't too often. Every time he pulls a new variety he brings it in to show me regardless of the dirt dripping onto the floor. I have the consolation of knowing that I shall be informed if any flowers are pulled.

The hoe captain just came in to have his second bee sting of the day treated. I think we are going to have to use a little diplomacy to see if we cannot induce the boss to move that last swarm farther from the strawberry patch.

And now the weed puller is wondering if I might have time to read the funnies to him. At the suggestion he go help Charles so he will finish sooner and have time for reading comics, he objects. In his opinion it would be best to wait until Charles has finished and then ask him.

The last ovenful of bread is done. Those tomato plants I forgot last night and the night before must not be neglected any longer. Maybe I can get two boys to help me so we can get them all transplanted before time to start the evening meal.

A L L day the little boys had been excited about it. Although they had retired earlier than usual the previous night, it had been difficult to go to sleep while thinking that tomorrow would be Grandma's birthday. Despite that they were up early the next morning. To them the day seemed endless, but at last they were told that they could get ready.

It had been hot and dusty. The youngest had been busy tearing down sparrow's nests. After he had taken a bath he looked dirtier than before because all the dust became wet. When he was sent back, he wailed that the water was too muddy. I looked and agreed with him. He drained the water out of the tub and turned on more water. That time his appearance began to suggest that there might be a chance of getting off all the muddy streaks. However, it took a third tub of water to get him reasonably clean.

While he and the others were dressing, I was packing dishes, spoons, and materials for making ice cream. I couldn't mix it and put it in the freezers as usual because someone else was furnishing the eggs and cream this time.

At last we were almost ready. For the third time, I unbuckled the youngest's belt and tucked his shirttail inside his overalls. The next time I suggested that he change to his sailor suit. After a complaint that he feared he would spill ice cream on it and it was so thin the cream would get him all wet, he changed to the sailor suit.

We climbed into the car. Everything had gone well except that somebody had dropped the picnic box and broken three dishes.

There were forty-eight people at the party and most of them seemed to be of the younger generation. But that was only because the noisy ones were the most in evidence; a count revealed that twenty-five adults were there.

The guest of honor knew her age this time. Last year she told the crowd she was 72, and I had to remind her that 1868 subtracted from 1939 leaves only 71. We visited with all. Then we devoured banana, raspberry, vanilla, and other kinds of ice cream.

Presently the noisy group became quiet. Cars began to leave. We followed their example. Two tired and sleepy small boys insisted on scraping some more cream out of the bottom of one of the freezers before they went to bed. They hadn't had much fun, they added. Perhaps they hadn't had much fun during the last half hour riding home, eating additional cream they didn't want, and getting into bed. But I'm quite sure they will be ready and eager to go to Grandma's birthday party again next year.

THE youngest was crying because he couldn't go to town with his dad and eldest brother. And when the youngest cries, he works at it with all his might. It was difficult to pretend I couldn't hear such loud, energetic howls. It was more than useless to remark that the two middle sons would have enjoyed going too, although they were not making any fuss about it.

Charles, my chief assistant, had to stay to help take the last batch of the day's canning of corn off the fire and to do the evening chores. The other lad had no particular duties that were pressing but this was a hurry-up trip and the boss didn't have time to be bothered with two inquisitive youngsters. The boss resented having to go almost as deeply as his three sons who didn't get to accompany him resented having to stay.

The corn had been set off the fire but the pressure wasn't down enough to remove it from the canner. There was no reason why I should stay in the kitchen where I couldn't keep from hearing my youngest son.

To the boy Bruce I remarked that I was going out to the garden to see if there were any ripe tomatoes and if more of the flowers had begun to blossom. He jumped up readily when I asked if he wanted to go along. At the door, I flung back a careless invitation to the weeper, which brought forth louder yells of woe. We sauntered slowly up the path and had reached the stone steps and started up them to the front yard before Irvin came out of the door. He caught up with us at the second step and wordlessly grasped my hand.

At the garden gate, I spied a burdock bearing burs of green with gay purple blossom tops. Right then and there, I made the first burdock bur basket I've made since I wore my hair in pigtails tied with blue ribbons that were forever getting lost. That healed the broken heart and stopped the sobs that had continued even after the howls had ceased.

While I hunted tomatoes, Irvin found more bright new burs for making baskets, stopping only long enough to admire the marigold blossoms that have appeared since the last rain. Just now he has thrust a bunch of them wadded into a ball in my hand as I sit trying to write.

Many times in the almost five years that we have lived here, my sons have informed me that every burdock has been cut. Always, however, there are some that have escaped the hoe. Maybe the bur baskets will get rid of those. A boy who is looking for burs to use for making baskets is apt to have much brighter eyesight than one looking for weeds to cut with the hoe.

Surely, if they are stripped of all their seed burs, sometime the burdocks will die even if they elude the languid hoer.

AGAIN he decides to run the lawn mower or any one of the numerous carts and wagons that he has constructed at different times. If he is too weary for such strenuous "resting" he busies himself with hammer, saw, and plane or the interesting task of taking bolts out of some of the old machinery on the junk pile and making new implements of his own invention, aided by two willing small boys, a very dull hacksaw, pliers, wrenches, and the indispensable hammer.

He insists that it is so dusty down in the field where he is harrowing that he can scarcely breathe. We have to concede that riding the harrow is a dirty task. I didn't say anything about it to him, but I've seen small boys play in very dusty places and at the same time indulge in much more violent exercise than standing on a harrow driving a three-horse team that requires frequent encouragement if it is to be kept going.

During the noon meal we were informed that the fieldwork would progress much more rapidly this afternoon. The driver of the small bay pony and the two big blacks announced that he had provided himself with an elm switch about six or eight feet long. Now it will be unnecessary to jump off the harrow, run alongside old Roger, hit him with the persuader, and hop back on the swiftly moving (at that moment) implement.

It seems to me that a stick so large as we described might be somewhat heavy and unwieldy for the young farmer to carry. But I don't presume to criticize my menfolks or to give them advice. I'm perfectly willing, but it doesn't do any good to waste words. Probably they take my advice as well as I do that they offer me. Haven't I been informed many, many times that it is unnecessary to sweep, mop, and dust? The house gets dirty again anyway. And if I didn't try to keep it clean it wouldn't be necessary to be so careful about tracking in mud and dirt.

Again, I've been told that I go to too much bother about meal preparation. It would be agreeable with them if I didn't bother about cooking meat, potatoes, and other vegetables every meal. We could get along with cake, pie, salad, and the like for some of the meals.

And why do I wash windows when I put up curtains so we can't see out of them? I guess I'm queer, too. I like to go out into the garden and pull weeds when I get tired. And some people rest by getting in the car and driving a few dozen miles. We are all queer. We don't have any reason to laugh at anybody for their notions and ways.

"ARE you Elizabeth?" she asked when I answered her knock at the door.

"Yes," I answered, not staring. At least I hope I wasn't staring.

"Then who am I?" was the surprising question that brought me out through the screen door and onto the porch. I know I was staring by then. A glance at the car by the side of the road showed only the farmer driver—no babies or children.

"You don't look like any of them," I blurted with my usual poise and tact. She didn't. Too old and tall for Maxine. Too young and not heavy enough for Myra. Too large for Marijo. Rapidly I thought of the various readers who had described themselves to me. It had to be somebody who had written a good many times over a long period of time or she wouldn't have bothered about coming to see us.

"Who is tall and bony?" she prompted, helpfully.

"That's Virginia, but she claims she's fat." I frowned. Virginia is in her twenties and my visitor wasn't trying to pretend to be youthful.

The car bothered me. The farmer sitting back of the steering wheel might be any of the husbands, for I don't have a very clear picture of many of them. It wasn't Cecil or Kenneth, I was sure. But it might be one of the Joes, Jims, Johns, C.W.'s, or J.T.'s, for all I knew. I have a pretty vague idea about most of the husbands. I believe I'd be more successful guessing the sons.

But the car was too—well—too nearly new to belong to any whose personal description didn't differ too much from that of my caller. Mrs. S. had emphasized her size and weight.

I had been cheated. I hadn't been told when the new car had been purchased. How could I guess that my visitor was the one who wrote, a scant eighteen months ago, "Believe it or not I am an expert at dodging the leaky places in the roof of the dear old car. Once I sat in a puddle of water all the way home from town. I'll wait to visit you until I have some other way of coming than hitchhiking." (Ah, the next sentence proves that I was warned and had no reason for complaint.) "We had planned to get something better to ride in with our next 'big bunch of spending money' but may have to use it for other purposes."

But I didn't guess and she had to tell me. I was disappointed because her youngest, who used to draw pictures and write scrawly letters for me, has grown to be a schoolboy and couldn't come.

And she forgot to look at the jail while she was here, she wrote afterward. Her husband walked right past it when he and the boss were hunting for a gate to lean on while they talked but no doubt he failed to recognize the imposing edifice. A car body of a vehicle that wasn't very big in the first place isn't very tall when it is taken off the chassis. Perhaps he saw the latter. The eldest made a cart out of it and usually it is in front of us no matter where we try to go.

But I'm glad she came even if I didn't get to see the artist and writer of the family and I'm sorry about the jail. The boss isn't, though. He doesn't take much pride in his son's architectural triumph. He says he is glad they didn't see it.

OUR long-legged Charles is thirteen years old today even though his parents have difficulty in realizing the fact. He is taller than his mother. Other parents who have tall sons will know the strange feeling that comes to one upon realizing that the boy is no longer a baby. He is taller than his elder brother, who will be fifteen next week. The eldest doesn't approve of that at all. It isn't fair for the insignificant being, who is to him what younger brothers have been to older brothers and sisters since the beginning of family life, to shoot up into prominence so suddenly.

But Charles isn't taller than his father. The boss was somewhat reluctant to submit to a measuring, although he did not admit it. He postponed the ordeal but at last we asked him when he couldn't plead lack of time for he was getting ready to rest for a few moments. To the disappointment of the one and the relief of his parents and big (?) brother we learned that the broad shouldered parent was taller than the slender son.

When a lad shoots up toward the ceiling very suddenly his parents become as helpless as they were during his first case of baby colic. What can be done about those long arms that protrude, if not for miles at least for inches, below the sleeves of the shirt and sweater bought only a few weeks ago? And the trousers that were too long at the beginning of the school year now seem undecided whether to stop at the knee or ankle and compromise by reaching halfway between. What can one do? A new suit purchased now would be too small two months hence. And the eldest could not bear to wear a hand-me-down cast off by a brother who ought, by rights, to be the smaller. It has been bad enough to have that younger brother be of equal height and almost as heavy as his senior brother for years and years. It isn't right for him to be taller and it would be an additional insult to have to wear his outgrown clothing.

There was no help for it. Our orator just had to make his speech at the contest attired in the eldest's new trousers and his own rather skimpy sweater. Somebody offered to lend him a suit to wear when he spoke at our neighboring city. She said many other boys had worn borrowed suits on such occasions; but Charles is rather an unlucky mortal and we agreed with him that he couldn't get there and back without tearing it, having somebody spill something upon it, or meeting with some totally unexpected happening that would ruin it.

There is a consolation of sorts. A boy who is hurrying so fast about his growing ought to be through with it very soon. Perhaps someday soon he will cease to outgrow his garments as soon as they are purchased. But parents are never satisfied. They'll complain about something else by then, I suppose.

SKIPPY, the four-year-old pup who owns this family, can boast of blue blood in his veins. Unlike Nig, the black setter, whose ancestors were all setters, Skippy can claim ancestry of many lines. In appearance he shows only his fox terrier and Eskimo dog blood but those who have seen his mother say she resembles one of her bulldog ancestors to some extent. His perseverance and inability to become discouraged at any task he undertakes are traits that he must have inherited from this branch of his family. Otherwise, Skippy is mostly fox terrier despite the fact that he loves cold weather and thinks the top of a snowdrift the most comfortable spot to rest.

Doubtless there is some rat terrier blood there too, for Skippy's sole purpose in life other than worshipping his master, assisting Nig with his groundhog digging, and other work a setter has to do is to find and destroy rats. To be sure, he enjoys bringing in the cows or horses when the eldest rides Ted after them but that, like the help he gives Nig, is merely a matter of pleasure. The hunting of rats, or mice if no more worthy game can be found, is a very serious business that requires all his attention until completed. If there is a rat under the brooder house or corncrib it would be just as impossible to get Skippy to leave it to chase cows or to eat as it would be to get Nig to desert a groundhog until its destruction is completed.

One Saturday morning Dick was very eager to get to the cornfield while Charles and Vaughn were home from school to help him. But Skippy found a rat and demanded the assistance of Dick and all four of his sons. The first I knew about the matter was when the fleeing rodent took refuge in the drain under the back porch. No amount of coaxing would induce either the dogs or our two younger sons to step back a few feet in order to be out of sight of the intended victim.

At last one end of the drain was stopped with a pair of worn overalls, and the old corn planter plate that serves as a strainer for the drain opening in the porch floor was removed and a pail of water was poured in. The swill pail was set over the drain opening instead of the usual corn planter plate and everybody ran to the open end of the drain to watch for Mr. Rat. One boy announced that the swill pail was moving. The boss ordered it moved so the rat could come forth to meet his doom. I did that and, to be more helpful, I opened the screen door and let the exceedingly wet creature out to meet the dogs and humans. That earned me a scolding, for the rat ran past them and crept between the rock wall and the side of the house. Digging was tried, and also barking and poking with a stick from above and below. It took two of us to hold the dogs while the others tried to scare the enemy out. There should have been two more to hold the two youngest sons but that wouldn't have left anyone to get the rat from his hiding place. The boss started to the barn two or three times. He was going to the field. He couldn't spend all day here if somebody was going to turn the rat out every time he got it where it could be killed.

At last the eldest ran for the pliers, took a firm grip on the protruding tail and brought to view the cause of our difficulties. Skippy did his part of the work and the cornpickers went on to the field not more than half or three-quarters of an hour late.

THERE have been complaints that Effie May and the dogs haven't been mentioned lately. Like all other young animals, including human ones, Effie May grew up; and like all others, with the exception of human ones, she ceased to be quite so much of a nuisance when she stopped being a baby. For a long time we haven't seen much of Effie May for she has been out in the pasture with the other cattle instead of in the yard, chicken lot, barn lot, hog pasture, or wherever she could be the most bother. This morning she came back to the barn and with her was a wobbly legged black calf. The boss says she is an accomplished kicker already although he has milked her but one time.

Yet, even though Effie May now is a two-year-old heifer with pretensions to dignity, I cannot forget past happenings. Two years ago, when she chewed the newly washed garments as they hung on the line and found various other mischievous things to do, she was just a calf and the only calf on the farm at that. Just the same, it is my ardent wish that she be kept out of the chicken lot, where hangs the clothesline on washdays of the future.

As for the dogs, I haven't liked to say much about them. They became very ill during the coldest weather of the winter.

Finally Nig died. Skippy, who hurt his back jumping out of a haymow door when he was a puppy, a few weeks ago again lost control of himself as he did when his back was hurt. This time he didn't recover in a few days. Days and weeks passed until Skippy was over his illness but he still found it almost impossible to walk or stand. He waxed fat from lack of exercise after he began to eat again. At last he began to improve slowly. When the ground was ice coated I found it difficult to walk since Skippy, glad to see me, tried to romp in front of me but made a sad failure of it.

With our rat catcher crippled, the rodents crowded into the barn. One day a bold rat came too near the quick jaws of our dog of many breeds. That cheered Skippy wonderfully. Wasn't he well now that he had killed a rat? It cheered Skippy's folks, too. We forgot his past faults and remembered only his skill as a rat destroyer.

Gradually the little dog has gained his sense of balance. Sometimes his treacherous back betrays him and he doesn't move at all or at least not where he had expected. Again he has declared war on the hated rats and is destroying every one he can find.

We miss our groundhog killer, Nig, the big black setter. But we are might glad that Skippy is well again, even though he is a cripple of sorts.

MY brother, my sister, and I have been staying with our mother down at her home. The first night it seemed rather queer to be there. It had been long years since I had spent a night there. The house seemed to be empty and still. Of course, the dad we miss so much wasn't there. That accounted for part of the strange feeling that our family was so small.

But that wasn't the only reason why, in spite of gladness to be home again and with our mother in her illness, the house seemed so empty to me. It seemed that the five other members of my family belonged there. No doubt my brother and sister felt the same way about the missing members of their families.

Early in the mornings, my brother and I went to our own homes. Once I stayed home all day; once I spent the afternoon. When the patient improved I came home and have been here two nights, driving down for a visit only in the evenings. But now I'm going back to stay all the time for a while. My sister is going to her home to do her washing and get some more of her things. She had come down intending to stay only one night instead of a week.

All summer my mother has planned to go home with my sister this fall; she will go as soon as she gets better. I'm always dreadfully homesick when my mother goes up there. When I can talk to her over the telephone or even when I know she is at my brother's house, close enough to return home every day that she is well enough, I feel differently. Then I know that if I have time I can slip into the old home for an hour or two, look at treasures of other days, and recall past happinesses. But when she is far away it seems that not only she but the old home is far away, too. If you have an old home or have had one, you will know how it is. Otherwise, it is useless to try to explain. I think you will understand that I'm hoping very much that she will be well enough to come and spend a few days with me before she goes on the longer trip.

Contradictory creatures, we humans, aren't we? It makes me homesick to have her away from the old home unless she is at my house. Then it doesn't seem so lonely for the old home to be empty because we could run down there any time and unlock the door. I'm not quite selfish enough to want her to come if it will make her too tired for the long trip she is so anxious to make. I'm not selfish enough to want her to miss that trip even though it will be very lonesome while she is gone.

Down here at my mother's the days are not quite the same as they are at our hillside dugout. One difference is that they are twenty-four hours long. Of course, at home we sometimes have twenty-four-hour days in times of illness, but even then some of us have night and day. But down here the only difference between day and night is that the nights are cooler and we have to have a light.

At 6 A.M. I give medicine, replenish the fire, write letters to some of the nearest relatives, pack lunches for the high school boys who will stop for them on their way to school, get breakfast for the invalid, encourage her to eat it, chat a moment with the boys as they bring me an armload of wood or a pail of water and then hurry on to school, eat my own breakfast, and wash the dishes when there is time.

The patient spent most of the hours at first, both day and night, in the chair because it was more comfortable than the bed. Then more of her daytime hours were spent in bed and more of the night hours in the chair. Lately, less and less time is spent in the chair.

At first it was very lonesome with only one large cat on the doorstep—no dog, no chickens, no pigs, no outside chores with the exception of fuel gathering. Kitty was highly pleased to have company. He had spent most of the summer there alone.

Then one Sunday morning my very homesick mother and my sister who was there for the day walked the short distance from my brother's home down to my mother's. By noon my mother was seriously ill. Of the twelve days that have passed since then I have spent two at my own home and two or three of the nights. My sister stayed until Friday and then went home, returning Thursday morning. Now I'll go home for a day or two.

There are five more cats on the doorstep. A mother and her family decided something needed to be done about the table scraps that were going to waste. The first cat didn't care for them after being used to a fresh meat diet. He turned up his nose at cake, bread and butter, cooked meat, and the like. Rats and mice made more aristocratic food. The five new cats are not so particular. Having them here helps. I don't miss old Rover and the cats who used to belong—at least not quite so much.

But mealtimes are lonesome. I eat at a corner of the table next to the stove. Grandpa's empty chair stands by the cupboard where he used to sit and talk while we were preparing meals. I could eat at my old place at the side of the table—but I don't. All the time I'm thinking, "That was Dad's place—and that was hers—and at the end sat my big brother until he went away and didn't come back—we other three children sat in these places— and whoever was the company at my left hand." Memory brings back dozens of long unseen faces when I look at the company place. No, I don't eat at my old place, since the others are not there to eat with me.

Yes, I'm a sob sister—in the kitchen. I have to be gay when I go back through the front room to the bedroom.

In January of 1940 my mother had an operation for cancer. Dick and the boys took me over to the back end of our east eighty in the bobsled. Dick helped me wade through the snow, and I walked down the track to the crossing by Uncle Frank McAlister's where I was met by my brother. I rode with him to the hospital in Ottumwa. I had walked only about a mile, but I suffered frosted hands, feet, and face in the icy wind.

A G A I N   I am home to spend a night.
   The youngest suggested that it would be a good plan for me to stay "quite a while" this time since I am here. But I am going back to my brother's home where the ambulance brought my mother yesterday. Then my sister can go home for a few days and later return to give me another vacation.

When I went back to my mother in the hospital last week the boss didn't take me to the railroad track in the sled as he had planned. We started that way, intending to go through our east eighty acres to the corner nearest the railroad, where neighbors who have cut their winter's fuel in our timber have a gap in the wire through which they drive with their loads of wood. Our only mishap was when the sled slipped over a stump hidden under the deep snow and refused to come loose until Barney and Old Roger had made a complete circle. Just as we gave up the sled slid off the obstruction and we plowed on merrily through the drifts.

We saw the pathetic little body of a quail that had frozen to death, perhaps during the night of our worst blizzard.

When we reached the north "line fence" we found the gap was hidden under a snowdrift that covered the fence posts. The snow had blown off our neighbor's field and been stopped by the fence. There was no choice. The horses couldn't wade through soft snow five or six feet deep and pull a sled after them. We had to walk, although it wasn't very pleasant.

Once over the fence and the drifts progress was somewhat easier, although the bitter cold wind took one's breath. It couldn't have been more than a quarter of a mile to the railway but it seemed ages before we came to its fence and plowed our way through the deep snow that had drifted over it. We floundered through the snow-filled ditch beside the track, and when we had gained the ties I went on alone to the crossing where the car was waiting. It wasn't very far for it was in sight from where we crossed the fence, but I was cold enough and tired enough that I think ten steps more would have been too many. How I envied the blossoming plants I saw in the windows of the warm houses we passed along the highway!

While I was gone the roads drifted full and were shoveled out again. The ambulance had to travel eight miles on the way out from Blakesburg to reach my brother's home, which is only two miles from town. Dick and Vaughn had broken our roads with the team and sled so they could go to town for groceries, and they met me and brought me home in the sled. Wrapped in the warm robe, I couldn't feel the cold air. The team may not have enjoyed the trip, but I found it much more pleasant than plunging through the drifts.

One of my friends in Blakesburg had said the boys could stay at her house when the weather became bad. When I came home from the hospital a few weeks later I found my sons had not stayed in town, since they thought their father would be needing them to help do the chores and take care of the two younger brothers. All the family were ill when I returned.

My mother lived until the last of September. I spent the last month with her down at the old home place. The boys rode their bikes to school and could bring us some groceries on their way home. One day it turned cool. My mother had to stay in bed; it was too cool to get her up in a chair. I was planning to ask the boys to get me something to burn in the kitchen stove when they stopped on their way home from school. But they didn't stop that night. Dick was baling hay, so they hurried straight home to help him. When they come past Grandma's they ride a little farther than usual, so this time they had taken a shortcut. That was on Friday. Mamma had to stay in bed until after the boys found some fuel for me on their way home Monday evening; I couldn't leave her to go outside to find something to burn.

One night she awoke and saw me sitting by the bed. She insisted that I get in bed and sleep, too. I was afraid to sleep, though, since she was so very ill. I pretended to be asleep until she began slumbering again.

THE boss is popping corn. Charles is reading a book. Vaughn is listening to a radio program. The little boys are eating popcorn and trying to keep from looking sleepy. I have just finished rereading three letters that came from *Tribune* readers. Isn't it strange that no letters come some days and then several come at once on other days?

It seems that we do have more girl readers than we thought. Requests are coming for a picture of the boss. I am proud to learn that a column I wrote seven years ago made one farm wife acquainted with the *Tribune,* and she and her family have read it ever since.

Here are the answers to some of the questions you asked. The youngest's name is Irvin. Moravia is our post office address but when I talk of the home town I mean Blakesburg, which is closer.

Yes, our house is on the west side of the road, built in the hillside almost at the top of the hill. That makes our front door in the east and the back door in the south side of our house.

The eldest likes to do carpenter work; tinker with any kind of machinery; draw pictures of landscapes, farmsteads, and the like; take care of the sheep and poultry; work in the field; and chop down trees. He thinks he would like to cook but he never has time to learn.

Charles is interested in geography, the newspaper sports page, milking, hunting wood and kindling, playing indoor games, reading everything he can get his hands on, and seeing that his mother doesn't do any of the work he claims as his own. His dad and big brother call him Pete. Both the big boys like the phonograph, the radio, and music of any kind, although they never have had an opportunity to take lessons so they could make music themselves.

The third boy went by the initials R.B. until he was a year old. Then the boys began calling him Bruce, his middle name. They had called my father Bruce until then, when they suddenly began calling him Grandpa. Finally I began calling the baby Bruce because the boys did, but the boss and a good many of the neighbors still call him by his initials. Bruce likes to read and play indoor games. He used to like to work, but he has gotten over that. No doubt he will soon outgrow his lazy streak. Most children go through that stage about the time they get over the contrary period.

The youngest wants to do whatever one of his big brothers is doing. He likes to work, but he thinks he is too big to be bossed. If we ask him to do something the answer is likely to be, "I don't want to do that" or "I don't feel like it." The boss calls him Earl, which is his middle name.

THERE is excitement in our household. Junior and Donald Wayne have moved from the house over by the schoolhouse to the house at the foot of the hill. For the first time our younger sons have company along the mile tramp from here to school.

It was a big day when Delene—the young lass who cut the foot out of Bruce's stocking when it escaped through a hole in his shoe during school hours one day—came back to school again after a year's absence. There was much talk in high-pitched voices when Delene brought a young relative to school with her.

He was a brother or cousin, they explained, and they were pretty sure he was going to stay in school, since he recited in reading class. But all of this was as nothing in comparison with knowledge that two of his schoolmates were to be very near neighbors.

The first day Junior and Donald Wayne went to school early, which was a great disappointment to the boys from this house. However, they came home together that night—the two six-year-olds running on ahead while their seniors followed at a more sedate pace.

"I waited in Donald Wayne's house until they came," explained Irvin. "He asked me." At my suggestion that it was best not to linger on the way from school but to come straight home, the subject was changed.

After they had gone to school—in the rain—the next morning I remembered that in the haste of getting wraps and overshoes collected I had forgotten to tell our socially minded son to pay no more calls on his return trips.

That evening they came home in high spirits. They had caught up with their new neighbors at the Soap Creek bridge and walked all the way to school with them. But, to my dismay, I learned that again Irvin had paid a call while waiting for his big brother. No, he hadn't removed his overshoes, for they hadn't been muddy. That seemed odd to me since there is a clay hill road between our neighbor's house and the schoolhouse. And his overshoes were dripping generous chunks of mud over our porch as he talked.

I don't know anything about hobbies. I've collected rocks, stamps, pencils, antiques, chewing gum wrappers, and various other things during my career. I've crocheted miles of cotton to the extent of making a bedspread. I have embroidered fancywork and things not so fancy. I've knitted socks and sweaters for soldiers and the neighbors' babies, and I wound up my orgy with a grand finale when I knitted a room-size rug that met with disaster after it had graced my dining room fewer months than it took me to knit it. You ought to see me drive nails.

I've cooked; baked; raised poultry, pet pigs, calves, and one bay colt; given and taken home demonstration lessons and piano lessons; worked at various jobs from telephone operator to bank bookkeeper; cut sprouts in the timber and fodder in the cornfield; picked corn; planted corn; plowed the sod for corn; led the stacker horse; ridden the rake; done the stacking; milked cows and helped grind and mix their feed; and arisen at 3 A.M. to ride miles in the big wagon with a small son on either side of me after loads of coal, arriving home at noon—or a bit later—tired, hungry, and black; and raised goldfish for sale. A few dozen other vocations have kept me busy most of my life.

But I never had a hobby. Whatever I was doing seemed the most important thing in the world until something happened to make it impossible for me to do it any longer, and then I found something else just as important and as engrossing. When I was rather young I thought I'd like to be a librarian, a bookkeeper, a lawyer, a college student, a writer, or an architect.

I drew the plans for the house in which we live. It suits the people who live in it but few others, so my architectural career will not include planning for others as I had dreamed at one time. As a lawyer in the home court here on the top of the hill I've met with indifferent success. My sons prefer to settle their disputes by force rather than by law, so a lawyer isn't needed in our domain.

The other vocations have been given due attention. I am qualified to discuss vocations, but I know nothing of hobbies.

AGAIN I am writing from the hospital, but this time I am not the patient. Although we clung to every hope, the youngest did have to have his mastoid operation after all.

He is a good little patient. His doctors tell us he is getting along very well indeed, although he is a sick little boy yet. In fact, if he had not been of such an uncomplaining nature we might have discovered his condition before it became so bad.

The last time we brought him to see the specialist we were told to take him to the hospital at once. Naturally I didn't go back home with Dick, although I had had no idea we would have to stay. After Dick had gone home I thought of some of my possessions that I could use to advantage. It didn't worry me too much that I had forgotten to ask the boss to bring them, for I didn't have much faith in the ability of the men of my family to find what would be needed.

That showed how much I knew about them. They came the next day—the boss, Vaughn, Charles, and a very dirty-faced Bruce. In a box they had brought my new black-and-white checked print dress that I made one day last week, my toothbrush, tooth powder, paper, envelopes, a washcloth, and a towel. Doesn't that prove that, like all women, I underestimated the abilities and the understanding of my menfolk?

But that wasn't all—they carried a heavy comforter and an Indian blanket to make my rocking-chair bed more comfortable these chilly nights. At their request I wrote a list of the things I'd like for them to bring the next day. So now I have my typewriter, clean handkerchiefs, a pair of cotton hose, and my faithful plow shoes.

When night comes, I don my print dress and my everyday hose and shoes, put the heavy comforter in the rocking chair, wrap myself up in it, and pull the blanket over me. Until some restless tossing or a moan from the bed of the small patient wakens me I forget that these rooms are not so warm at night as they are in daytime. In fact, I forget I am not in bed until my neck begins to ache because I have neglected to hold up my head.

The thought of it makes me sleepy. The snores of the youngest make me sleepier. Do you suppose seven-thirty would be too early for me to go to bed? Maybe it would, but I'm not going to bed. I'm going to the rocking chair just as soon as I can slip into the checked dress.

ON this farm, Saturdays are eventful days. Last Saturday was no exception. Since we are not permitted to have the whole page, there will not be room to tell of the whole day's happenings. We'll skip as much as we can.

I sent Bruce to the mailbox with some letters. He returned without waiting for the mail.

"Junior and Donald Wayne said they were coming up after dinner," he announced.

"Did you stop down there again?" I demanded.

"Well, yes. I just went in the house a minute."

"Don't you think their mother gets tired of having you there *all* the time?"

"I don't know. They said they were coming up to see Irvin."

Presently he went back after the mail and lost a letter. I went back to help him hunt for it, but we didn't find it because a neighbor had picked it up and returned it to us later as he was passing. Neither my work nor my resting seemed to progress at all. Just as dinner was on the table came a knock at the door. Seeing a small head through the glass, I sent Bruce to open the door. He did and stood there, speechless.

"Tell them to come in," I suggested. Still wordless, he stepped back and two shy boys entered.

"Well, we haven't had dinner yet. Did you come to eat with us?" asked my polite young son. They shook their heads.

"Why don't you take them upstairs?" I guessed the shyness would disappear if there were no big folks around. My theory proved to be correct if one may judge by the sounds that issued from upstairs.

Irvin, not being able to eat since his operation, entertained the visitors while his next elder brother ate a small fraction of what would have been his meal had he not been in a hurry.

After noon, I went upstairs to find trucks, cars, and toys of all kinds all over the floors. The fire truck had been taken outside to see how high it would shoot the water. Rook was being played. I helped Donald Wayne and Irvin with their discarding whenever one of them got the bid.

The three well boys kept running outside to play, which annoyed Irvin. Twice he locked them outside as punishment. When Donald Wayne and Junior asked questions about the furnace I told Bruce to show it to them. Irvin slammed the door between the dining room and furnace room and locked the one between the kitchen and laundry. The cook let two boys out through the kitchen, but the frightened Donald Wayne came out through the other door, thin plywood as it is, despite its snap catch. Luckily, the screws to one hinge came out before the door broke.

I just wonder how those boys' mother—with two babies—manages when my sons call at her house? I think it is about my turn to herd the four of them for a while. She had her share with three of them when Irvin was in the hospital.

V E R Y early this morning Dick and Vaughn left for the other farm with the back seat and all available storage space in the car filled with bricks and various tools they might need in repairing the cistern wall. Yesterday they took cement and sand, our best hoe, the spade, and some pails.

When they came back last night, I was quite disappointed to learn they had spent the day cleaning out the cistern and hadn't even started on the dangerous task of rebuilding the tumbling walls. It has been with difficulty that I've kept myself from wishing that the walls might have tumbled down during the night. That would mean digging a new cistern in another location, much less hazardous work than repairing one that is apt to cave in at any moment.

If there had been room in the car I might have accompanied them. Then when there is no longer any danger I would know about it. So long as I'm twenty-odd miles away I have to keep my eyes open all the time. If I dare to shut them I see things I don't like to see or imagine. But too much paraphernalia was needed. Room couldn't be made for me and for the three boys who might have wished to go if I went.

Farm workers don't think much about dangerous tasks since it is so seldom that they have a safe one. But I hadn't managed to hide my uneasiness about the absent ones. A while ago the two younger boys were worrying a bit during a pause in their play.

"My, we'll have a time—quite a time—if they both get killed in that well," remarked one.

"Yes, we'll have a big time," replied the other in a sad tone.

"It would be a horrible time, just horrible," added the first speaker, as he resumed his playing and proceeded to forget all about the matter.

Wives and mothers aren't very good at voicing their worries about "big times" and "horrible times" they fear may come to them, but their worrying is persistent and steady. The younger masculine element can worry wholeheartedly for half a minute and then have a good time playing or quarreling the rest of the day.

A T the Corn Carnival last fall I told Lloyd's mother I wished she had a telephone so that I could call her some afternoon to see if she would go with me to visit school. She told me to write a note, send it to school by the small sons, and her son would bring it to her. But I didn't write a note. There were afternoons that I could have gone, but I never knew it far enough ahead of time to send the note to school the previous day.

When I was soliciting for Red Cross membership, she asked me when we were going to visit school. I didn't know. The forecast was for rain and the next day was a bread baking day. I might not get it baked in time to get away for the afternoon. However, that evening we didn't eat much bread for supper. I decided the baking could wait another day.

The next morning was clear and pleasant with no sign of rain. I remarked that I could have gone to school that day, in fact, it would be possible to send a card to my neighbor by the mailman but there would be no way of hearing from her if she couldn't come. Irvin heard me talking. At his insistence I wrote the card and he hurried to the mailbox, promising to bring back the mail to save me the trip so that I wouldn't be too tired to walk the mile to school. When he brought the mail, he informed me the mail carrier said he would put the card right in the box.

So we visited school. Until recess I had to sit in the small seat in the front row with Irvin. That young man was rather disappointed when I chose a larger seat for the after-recess period.

He didn't waste time brooding over my desertion of him. He hurried to get his lesson studied and then asked the teacher if it wasn't about time for him to read. Perhaps it was or perhaps the teacher understood that his youngest pupil was eager to show his mother how smart he was, for the boy was permitted to stand up by the desk and read about the pig that refused to jump over the stile. Irvin had a very proud grin on his face, but the poor little fifth grader was so excited about having a relative at school that he had some trouble. When he had finished writing his theme for English—I don't know the subject but he asked the teacher how to spell argument—he folded the paper so tightly that he tore it as he creased it. And then, in spelling class he missed a word, to his everlasting shame. I didn't feel that it was such a disgrace, but perhaps I would have felt differently when I was in the fifth grade.

When a visit to school causes so much happiness and excitement, it does seem that mothers might spend more than one afternoon there each year. We could. Why don't we?

My own health was not very good during this entire period. I had an operation in 1937. In the one week in April 1939 between the deaths of Dick's mother and his father, I suffered a heart attack and was nearly incapacitated for several months thereafter.

In the spring of 1942 I was back in the hospital for a long postponed operation. I expected the children would have measles when I got home from the hospital, for they had had mumps, whooping cough, flu, and even pinkeye on my other homecomings. Somehow we got safely through the graduation of the class of 1942. Charles had measles and had to miss the senior banquet but insisted on going to the commencement exercises, although he was very weak and pale by the time they were over. When we returned home Vaughn, who went to the banquet but had to miss graduation, was out of bed trying to quiet his two younger brothers who were delirious with a high fever that comes to measles victims just before they break out. Vaughn went back to bed and left me to take care of the latest patients. He was too ill to inquire how the graduation went off without him.

10

The Family No Longer Intact

This chapter covers the period from the fall of 1942 until the end of my career as a newspaper columnist in February 1951. Those years saw great changes in the makeup of the Faber family. Since Irvin's birth in 1934 there had been six of us in the family. Except for those times when one of us was in the hospital or staying briefly with a relative, there were six of us at home every night.

In September 1942 Charles went away to school. Both he and Vaughn were in the service during World War II. Bruce went away to school in 1949. By 1951 there were only three of us at home—Dick, Irvin, and I. Vaughn and Charles had both married by then and I had acquired two daughters-in-law and three grandchildren.

At the age of fifteen Charles went to Coe College in Cedar Rapids on a scholarship. He worked at various jobs to earn his board and room. Vaughn didn't go to college. Because of the war he felt that he should enlist in the army. He failed the physical time after time but he kept trying. As Charles was only fifteen he knew he couldn't enlist, but when he became seventeen he joined the Navy. It wasn't yet the end of his second year at Coe, but his grades were good enough that he received full credit for the sophomore year. Shortly after this the army finally accepted Vaughn's repeated offers of his services.

In Irvin's last year at country school our school on the hill was closed and he had to walk to Center School. Bruce went to high school at Moravia; the first year he had to walk one mile to get on the bus. Sometimes when the roads were bad it didn't come. Then, after waiting, he would come home at noon, cold and wet from the snow or rain. One week he had to miss school because the roads were bad and the bus didn't come. After that he stayed with friends in town when the roads were too bad for the bus. After Irvin started to high school the bus came to our house, so there was no more walking. We now had a graveled road that was usually open. What a blessing to farm families school buses and all-weather roads are!

During the war years Charles was stationed at Farragut Naval Base, Treasure Island, Princeton University, and the University of Illinois. His sea duty was on an aircraft carrier escort that made several trips between California and Hawaii.

Vaughn's service stint was somewhat more dangerous. He served in the Philippines and was preparing for the invasion of Japan at the time of V-J day. Afterward he served in the army of occupation in Japan. Vaughn's trip back to the States became a long journey, for the typhoons to be avoided took much longer than usual. They ran out of food. Vaughn had an enormous appetite the first few weeks after his return.

After boot camp Charles came home for a scant twenty-three hours with us before returning to the naval base to be assigned to a ship. It was a time when many of our ships were being sunk. We were afraid it might be his last trip home. It was too sad a time for tears. I have not been able to cry at funerals of my parents or other loved ones. It is a feeling of shock and helplessness. When Vaughn left to be sent overseas with the army shortly thereafter, there was again only the terrible emptiness and the feeling that this was good-bye forever.

One day I went out to the garden. A huge snake had crept up one of the raspberry vines to a brown thrush's nest. Already the baby birds were dead from the loathsome fluid the snake had used to envelop and kill them before swallowing them. The mother flew about uttering piteous cries. Then I cried—not only for the mother bird, but for all the mothers whose offspring were at the mercy of the enemy—helpless like the baby birds, helpless like the mother bird.

Once when Sam Byrum was working for a young neighbor the baby of the household, a little girl of one or two years, died of the measles. "The silly mother didn't seem to care at all. She didn't even cry," said Sam. "But the next day it rained and she went out and found one of her little turkeys had drowned. She brought it in and cried over it, although she hadn't cared at all when the little girl died."

I wasn't very old when I heard that story, but even then I had the feeling that the mother was crying over the baby, as helpless against the disease as the turkey against the storm, when the turkey died.

During the war years I wrote of shortages of sugar, tires, clothing sizes for twelve- or fifteen-year-old boys, and of almost anything except the war itself. Readers wrote about their sons on ships and in foxholes, but I found it very difficult to write of Vaughn in the Philippines after hearing on the kitchen radio each morning of another soldier on Luzon being found with his throat cut during the night or of more ships being sunk in the Pacific or Atlantic. Instead I wrote of Charles's outgrown jacket, still as good as new, being stolen the first time Bruce wore it to school.

I wrote of going to hog sales and of writing pedigrees and of our sales out in the barn. I wrote of using honey as a substitute for sugar, of our tractor catching on fire and our difficulty in getting new tires to replace the burned ones. I didn't write about the war.

A selection of columns from this period follows. As compared to the previous chapters, fewer columns here are from the *Tribune* and more are from the Centerville, Moravia, Albia, and Blakesburg papers.

THIS is another of those cool August mornings. We can appreciate cool August mornings more than any other, for the coolness is welcome before the heat of the noonday sun.

The boy who is to go to the mailbox in fifteen more minutes is complaining that it is too cold. He sought refuge on the dining room couch. An elder brother pulled the blanket off him. He arose with reluctance and is now eating his breakfast with a pained look on his face.

It may be too cold for a barefoot boy to enjoy the trip down the hill this morning, but I am sure he will offer no objections if someone mentions going to the swimming hole this afternoon. At noon yesterday he confided that the water had been pretty cold in the morning but he thought it would warm up quite a bit by the time he got over there again.

Adults have little room to snicker at the youngsters. Circumstances change our feelings about matters, too, even though we might not go swimming when it is too cold to go to the mailbox. Yet sometimes we're too tired to do something we dislike to do but can go ahead with no complaints at something we want very much to do.

WE have looked over the school clothes and it has been decided that the youngest has enough shirts outgrown by Bruce and of his own, while the latter worthy gentleman has enough shirts outgrown by his two elder brothers. Each boy will have to have another pair of overalls before August 31, and some more socks will be needed unless the two big brothers decide to hand down some of theirs that fit too snugly.

Vaughn isn't worrying about school. He prefers to stay home and see that the tractor gets the proper attention. College doesn't sound interesting to him.

Charles has two new suitcases, a laundry shipping case, towels, blankets, shirts, sweaters, trousers, and goodness knows what all ready to go and a list of things to buy when he gets through threshing and collects his wages. He is counting the weeks, and his mother is trying to keep from counting them. Thus it would appear that we are almost ready for school.

But just now vacation is with us yet and we are trying to make the most of it. Today may be the last day the visiting cousins are with us. Their daddy is expected to drive in from Ohio tonight or early in the morning, and they will be on their way to the new air depot in Dakota.

There is much playing to be done. The youngest son and the boy cousin are hampered somewhat by the girl cousin. The boys, when reproached because they hadn't allowed her to play with them, said that they were working in the junkyard, and women never worked in junkyards. When they gave Barbara Jean the junkyard for her own and began to play with toy trucks, she wanted one of them. Presently Irvin gave her his truck, and the boys went to some of their other playing that was needing attention. Barbara Jean followed and came back with sawdust in her eyes.

Wayne had to sit in a chair. Irvin confessed that he threw a very small amount of sawdust, too. I suggested that he carry in six armloads of wood. His face was very red as he complied. When Wayne had finished his time in the quiet seat, he came to hunt for Irvin. That was lucky for Irvin, for Wayne carried in one armload of wood for him. I hurried upstairs before they entered the house; I was afraid I might not look as stern and forbidding as becomes a woman in the presence of two culprits who have been throwing sawdust at a lady.

The boys went back to play. "I'm going out and tease the boys some more, so they will throw sawdust at me again," murmured Barbara Jean.

"If you do you will carry in the wood this time," decreed her mother.

Once more I hear happy voices. Evidently the lady, who couldn't play while the gentlemen were being punished because she had no one to play with her, as well as the two lads are making up for time lost. Night will come all too soon.

While all the excitement of going to the new home may make the visiting cousins forget the past weeks, I am sure Irvin is going to miss the visitors very much.

THE college student came home unexpectedly last Thursday evening, just as I was wondering if I could wait twenty-seven more days until Thanksgiving to see him again. Somehow Friday and Saturday slipped away, and here it is Saturday evening with two columns to be written before Monday's mail. Perhaps if the men of the family hadn't gone to the old hometown for the regular Saturday night visit, the writing might have waited until after Charles returns to Coe Sunday afternoon. Even with half the family gone, it is somewhat difficult to write with the radio on the desk blaring out "Truth or Consequences" for the entertainment of the two youngest sons.

But now that Charles has gone to town to see his high school classmates of last year and his mother has his washing and ironing done, it might be wise to pound the old typewriter while trying to think of what to have for tomorrow's noon meal. It takes a great deal to feed a student home for the weekend. I had expected that—I, too, have eaten dormitory and restaurant meals. But this particular student worked until 11 P.M. Wednesday, rose too late for breakfast before class, left his last class in time to buy a ticket and two candy bars to take the place of a noon meal, and scrambled on the bus. No wonder "Is supper ready?" was his greeting as he walked in the door. Luckily it was ready, and the boy who had had only two candy bars in twenty-four hours had to wait no longer. Lucky for him, too, that motorists feel very kindly toward hitchhiking schoolboys, so he didn't have to walk that twenty miles from the bus depot. And lucky for both the boy and the cook that she had cooked enough potatoes to have enough left for warming up for the noon meal the next day. Needless to say, she peeled more for the next day's dinner and again for supper.

T H E visiting cousins have gone on their way to their new home, and the two little boys left playing alone are very quiet. Three boys can make an unearthly noise, but when two little boys are lonesome for the one who has left they can think of little shouting to do.

When there are three, two of them are likely to need to talk at the same time, and it is necessary to shout very loud in order to be heard. Then there is the necessary business of tormenting one lad and making him see that he is not so good as the other two. If he whines a bit it makes it all the more entrancing to get the best of him at every opportunity. When there are only two there is little incentive to try anything of this nature, for a boy runs the risk of offending his playmate and having to play alone.

At frequent intervals the playing is interrupted while Irvin goes to lead the hayfork horse as another load of hay is put in the barn. He had hoped that school would start before this crop of hay was ready to be cut because there are too many thistles along the horse's path and too much playing to be done at the house.

Bruce is a cripple at present. He stepped on a honey locust thorn and came to see me for aid and sympathy. As I tugged with all my might to pull out the huge thorn, I knew just how the hired girl felt the time she had to pull a nail out of my foot; it was very stubborn about coming out through the foot and the shoe it had entered so easily. It is easier to bear the pain of being hurt than to have to hurt someone else when necessary.

Bruce has to limp. He isn't crippled enough to interfere with his playing to any noticeable extent, but it does bother his work a great deal. The limp becomes much more pronounced when he goes after a pail of water or when he has to make a trip down the hill to the mailbox. And if he has to pick up a basket of corncobs he can hardly walk at all. Digging potatoes and cutting weeds have been entirely out of the picture. He can't do either of them until he is well again.

However, playing ball, hide-and-seek, or any other of several forms of exercise seem to help him in a most remarkable manner. In all fairness, I'll have to admit that he does limp when he runs about his play. But what makes me so sure that playing is healing instead of hurtful is the fact that he can play without whining or complaining about his sore foot.

This confirms my belief that playing is very good for boys, although work doesn't hurt them so much as they would have their parents think.

YESTERDAY Dick brought Brooke and Barney in from the pasture and spent some time repairing harness. This may be the machine age, but when snow comes and there are cattle to be fed the horses come in rather handy.

Of course it is a nuisance to get off the tractor and shut the pasture gate every time we go to or come back from the fields but there is nothing else to do, with the horses out of sight when we go through the gate but Johnny-on-the-spot within a few minutes if we leave it open. We haven't saddled Bill for a long time. When a riding horse is needed, there isn't anything to take the place of one. I guess this farm will keep a team and a saddle horse for a while before we go too modern.

Sixty-four addressed and stamped cards are lying on the desk ready to be mailed to the sixty-four families in the township who haven't sent their Christmas seal money yet this year. Your farm woman heaves a sigh of relief each year when she gets those reminder cards in the mail. And it never fails that the Christmas seal money comes from some of those people in the same mail that the reminders are posted. I always feel that some money has been wasted for stamps that might have been used to fight disease, but as usual I have waited three days past the time for sending out the reminders.

Most of the Christmas cards that are to be sent have been addressed and mailed with the clean white space filled with my peculiar scrawl on many of them. Since we hear from these friends and relatives only once a year it is almost impossible to resist scrawling a line or more on each of them.

When we were urged, via the newspapers, to get our Christmas shopping done in time to get our packages in the mail by December 10, I resolved to get it done at once. If I can't fire a gun at the enemy I can be patriotic in other ways. However, I can think of no greater test of patriotism than to be asked to get ready for Yuletide ahead of time. Usually I'm lucky if I am ready for it by the beginning of the New Year.

I made my usual New Year's resolution last year—the one about making Christmas gifts and doing Christmas shopping in spring and summer before the busy autumn season arrives. I did make a few things and started some others that may be finished by Christmas of 1945 or 1950.

Evidently everyone has not been so slow. Today the mailman brought a package—and such a package. I didn't wait until Christmas to open it. There have been times when I surprised myself by exhibiting that much fortitude, but today wasn't one of them. This time I had had a hint about the contents. Iva had written something about making a smock for herself and one for me. Also she had explained that the smallest of the aprons was chosen by her youngest son because he thought I would like the color. (I deduced that it was her private opinion that it was a bit too loud.) That lad knows my provincial taste. I liked it very much. The boss proclaimed that it was the prettiest of all, even nicer than the pink one I kept trying on every few minutes.

Of course you are more interested in Iva's letter than in what she sent me. As usual her letter contained a request that it not be printed. Her soldier and her marine remain at different battle fronts. Her college son has spent one weekend at home this fall. Like our schoolboy, he came in uniform, making his young brother strut with pride and his parents feel rather shaky and helpless. She inquired about the other readers' soldiers, sailors, and marines but I can't tell her much about them. Like Iva, most of the mothers of servicemen have to do nearly all their letter writing to their sons.

THIS is another of those mornings when every tree and every shrub is a picture no painting could equal. Probably it doesn't look so picturesque to Vaughn, who is picking corn for a neighbor. A corn picker would just as soon not see the cornstalks and shucks decorated with beautiful white snow. The Christmaslike scene appeals only to those who can remain indoors.

When Dick came back from the mailbox with a frosted face I began to wonder about Bruce, who is prone to linger absentmindedly and watch anything that may be interesting to a ten-year-old mind. Let us hope that he remembered to hurry over the hills to his destination.

Perhaps it was a good thing that Irvin decided at the last moment he didn't feel like going. He said he would like to go, but he didn't believe he had better. He hasn't been very sick, but he has had to miss a few days of school, and twice when he did start back he came home feeling very much under the weather. It would have been better if we had kept him out for several days the first time and he might not have had to miss any more at all.

But since I do not have to go to school or to the cornfield, I can enjoy the view. It appeals to me much more because Irvin is here and the house is not empty. There are a multitude of tracks in the clean whiteness of the mammoth rug in our backyard. At one time I enjoyed an unbroken expanse of snow-covered ground and regretted that we had to break paths to spoil its perfection. But since I have become a grown-up I like to see the paths to the barn, garage, hen house, machine shed, and across the road to the sheep shed; Bruce's tracks on the way to school; and the footprints of Skippy and the cats. There have been many lonely days since Irvin became old enough to go to school. With the tracks in the snow this farm doesn't seem quite so uninhabited when I am here alone.

FOR several years it has been the custom of readers of this column to make New Year's *voeux* or wishes for their friends and for the other readers whose letters have appeared here. How many of you remember how this custom originated? I knew Lila would remember, but how about the rest of you?

It began when I told the story of a devout little French girl who went with her friend to a little village church to say her New Year's *voeux*; after she came home she sat down and wrote to tell me that she had not forgotten me on this important occasion.

Jeanne's father had been killed in World War I. She supported her mother and grandmother by working in a clothing shop. When she grew up she became the wife of Antoine and went to Alexandria, Egypt, to live. There Antoine was an employee of the French bank. Life in Egypt was very strange to Jeanne, who was accustomed to work. There European women did no work. Everything was done by servants. Later, Antoine was transferred to Paris.

Soon after this I received two black-bordered envelopes within a few months of each other, addressed in a masculine hand. The letters within were in Jeanne's handwriting, though. She had lost her mother and her grandmother. She wrote that these losses left her without any family at all but that her husband still had all of his, which made it very nice for them. Also she wished me to make some inquiries about a silver fox fur that her husband had promised to buy for her.

The next news from Jeanne told of the birth of a daughter. She expressed the hope that her small Jacqueline might some day study English and write to my sons who would be studying French.

But again war came to her homeland. No word has come from her since the conflict began. All these long months I have been wondering about Jeanne and her husband and daughter.

Perhaps Antoine was a soldier as was Jeanne's father. I wished that there might be some way of getting Jeanne and her daughter to America. They might have gone to her home village, where she would have friends and where I hoped the land was not occupied by the enemy.

But now all of France is occupied. This year shall we save all our New Year's *voeux* (prayers and wishes) for Jeanne and all those in her homeland and ours who are endangered by this conflict? We needn't wait until January first. Will you remember her for me when you make your *voeux*?

T HE house reeks of perfume and sachet powder. There is a reason. We have an agent in our family. I advised against undertaking such a vocation, but mothers are old fogies who can't understand how important it is for a man to earn his own money in some more colorful way than by drying dishes, pumping water, and picking up cobs.

As I understand it, Bruce is a salve agent. But he has other products to sell. The sachet powder is, I believe, some sort of a premium. Bruce is inclined to believe it is really flower seed instead of sachet powder. It does have blossoms on the envelopes. It was a rather crestfallen agent who learned that he had sold two boxes of salve with free flower seed, only to learn it wasn't flower seed at all. In fact, he confided to me that he spilled some out of the envelope he was delivering to his teacher and it looked like sawdust, which proved it must be flower seed and not that other stuff after all.

At first all went smoothly for the new salesman. He had visions of ordering more of the product and obtaining a bicycle instead of a camera. I said nothing. His first order wasn't all sold yet, so there was no need to forbid the second order unless he advanced far enough to be ready for it. Nor does it seem necessary to issue any maternal mandates. There are four bottles of perfume, three boxes of salve, and the seven free packets of flower seed or sachet powder or whatever left.

As yet, Bruce has not despaired. There are a few houses in the neighborhood he hasn't canvassed; he can return to the house where he found no one at home and it is quite possible he may be able to convince his mother that it isn't too far to walk to some of the other houses he wants to visit. Feeling that he has his other parent's disapproval, our young businessman has neither asked his advice about where to go nor has he asked him if he would like to be a purchaser. Outwardly, the salesman has showed no despair at the sight of his unsold stock. But during the last two nights he has been in so much pain that he was unable to sleep.

I can understand that. When I was eight, his age, I was too big to cry because Blackie and her kittens had to be executed for her crime of eating chickens, but I suffered terrific headaches every night for a week. Actually, I did have headaches; it wasn't just a dream about the cat and kittens that woke me. And I'm sure Bruce does have a stomachache even though he may have been having a dream about trying to sell salve and perfume just before he wakes. But I notice the stomachache, like my headache, disappears when daylight arrives.

OF course we went to the Corn Carnival. We didn't get much work done, and when we returned about midnight Saturday evening we found a house that looked as if people had been eating and sleeping in it but nobody had been keeping it. But it was worth it to Bruce and Irvin, who rode the Ferris wheel and the merry-go-round, watched the programs, and took a great delight in the antics of the various barkers on the midway. The unlucky boy was lucky for once in his life. Saturday evening after we had been home for supper we hurried back to town. No sooner had we arrived than Bruce announced that he had left his purse at home, with all his three nickels in it. I loaned him a dime, hoping he would spend it before he lost it.

As soon as he left I began to doubt that he had left the purse at home. It didn't seem possible that he could have spent the whole afternoon without losing it. No doubt he had lost it without noticing the loss. I was sure of that when an announcement was made that a purse had been found.

After the program I hunted for Bruce but he was not to be found. So I went up to the platform and asked if the purse that had been found was a small brown zipper purse with three nickels in it. They gave it to me without further description, although I might have added the fact that it was somewhat worn and faded since it had gone through the washing machine in Bruce's overalls once. When I met the boy I asked him just where he had left his purse at home.

"Why, on the library table—I think," he replied, getting slower and slower as he neared the end of his sentence. His mouth fell open as I handed him the purse, and he was rendered quite speechless.

The boys had a good time, and I'm sure the head farmer enjoyed himself, even though he may know more people in the Moravia vicinity than in his wife's hometown.

Did I have a good time? What do you think? I met friends and relatives not often seen. A schoolteacher I had seen only once in the last quarter of a century, old neighbors who had been gone longer than that, new neighbors upon whom we've been too negligent to call—not through indifference but because I'm such a poor efficiency expert that I haven't learned how to budget my time for visiting. Cousins and my parents' cousins, my friends and my parents' friends, chance acquaintances I don't know very well but whom I'd enjoy knowing better, strangers who smiled their indulgence when I bumped into them, the children of old friends and schoolmates, people I like and people I don't like, people who like me and people who don't, and even the tightrope walker and her daughter were among the people who made the day what a celebration in the hometown is to anyone.

If sometimes the thought intruded that many of the familiar faces were missing; that of those who ate the noon meal together at the first Corn Carnival, eight are no longer with us; and that many of the old friends have grown feeble, I rejoiced that one can have happy memories rather than feel sad that today is not yesterday. I talked to people who talked with my ancestors who left this earth before I arrived and no doubt with some who will be talking to my descendants long after I have ceased going to Corn Carnivals. In fact, I had the same kind of day you Moravians have at the Fall Festival those years when an unusually large number of those you used to know come back and shake your hand.

May the Corn Carnivals and Fall Festivals last a long time, and may we have a land of peace and plenty in which to enjoy them.

SATURDAY afternoon with the farm family in town:

"Mother, Mother, you gotta dime?"

"No, I haven't. I'm sorry."

"Aw. Hey, Mother, you gotta nickel?"

"I'll look, but I don't believe I have. No."

"Say, Mother, you gotta penny?"

"I'm afraid not today."

"Dad, Dad. You gotta dime?"

"Why?"

"I wanta buy something. You gotta dime, Dad?"

"No."

"You gotta nickel, Dad?"

"No."

"Oh. Say have you got a penny, Dad?"

"Here."

"Thanks. I'll be back in a minute."

THIS morning I read in the paper of parents who made a surprise visit to their son's training camp at exactly the same time their son went home to surprise them. I made up my mind that I'm not going to try to surprise either of my servicemen sons. It would be a very poor surprise to both parents and sons to find the front door of the old home place locked and the army cot and navy bunk empty. I don't like surprise visits anyway. Too many times when relatives have tried to surprise me they have picked the only day in a fortnight that I had been away from home.

Of course, I'm just a sentimental old woman, but I couldn't be very happy when I saw the younger sons taking the rubber tires off the old coaster wagon that has been in the family these many years. To be sure I want to win the war, and I want to see Uncle Sam get every piece of scrap rubber we can spare, and the wagon is gone with only the wornout wheels remaining, so no practical person can understand why I felt sad about it. Perhaps there are other softies who will understand about that and also the queer feeling in my chest when the rubber goose and elephant, dilapidated as they were by the cutting of many small teeth upon them, went to help win the war.

THE third son of this family was born under an unlucky star. The only time in his life that he met with luck was when he found a dime in the potato patch last July when he was digging potatoes. Last year at the Fall Festival (Moravia) he lost a penny, on the Fourth of July he lost a dime, and Friday night at this year's Corn Carnival he lost his purse containing his entire fortune of fifteen cents. Worse than that he lost his family, and after hunting for us for, and we quote, "four or five hours" he became so weary he went to the car and waited four or five more hours before any of us came to take him home. He didn't get to ride on anything or see anything or get anything to eat or

drink. In fact, the only "fun" he had was "talking to the gover-
nor" with whom, he informed us, he became very good friends.

However, it hasn't made a pessimist out of our third son—
not our Bruce. On Saturday morning he told his younger brother
his plan, eyes gleaming with hope.

"You go get the mail; bring in the wood, cobs, and old shingles for kindling; and pump the water and I'll do *all* the rest of
the work."

That left only the dish drying. It was a beautiful scheme. But
it didn't work. Irvin brought the mail and dried the dishes, but
he insisted upon some help with the rest of it.

After writing that, I searched the car and found the missing
purse where the tearful youngster had shed his coat during the
long wait for his folks. He had looked in the car himself with his
usual success in finding things. Perhaps it would have been better to wait until Monday before finding the lost fortune, since it
had to be spent on Saturday night and now is lost forever.

The State Fair is over. The Fall Festival is over. For us, the
family reunions are over, although we didn't manage to attend
very many of them. Soon the Corn Carnival will be over. Maybe
I can get the furniture dusted.

VAUGHN helped put up the Christmas tree in one corner
of the library before he left to shoulder his gun. Then he
went away the week before Christmas. He didn't expect to
get back for the holidays, of course; nobody expected that. So
somehow the mother of the family doesn't feel as if we had had
Christmas yet; and the pathetic little tree with its shabby orna-
ments that have adorned many a tree in happier times stands
waiting in the corner of the library. Mothers are very foolish
creatures! They know it, but that doesn't make them any less
sentimental. If you wonder why it does any good for the tree to
wait in the corner for the two absent lads, it will do no good to
ask. Your Soap Creeker doesn't know, but there it stands.

Doubtless many of you were very glad to learn that the thing
between "and" and "or" is a *virgule* and not a *solidus* as some
persons have mistakenly assumed. At least the General Assembly
accomplished that much. I'm sure life will be much more worth
living for the average Iowan now that that has been settled. So
whether or not those legislators who want to repeal the and/or
that has occupied a prominent place in the Iowa code are success-

ful, it was worth the time to go to the polls to vote for our candidates that we might learn that the / between "and" and "or" is a what-you-call-it instead of that other word.

Now that that weighty matter has been settled let us hope they can do something to help the small boys who are trying to take the place of their older fighting brothers. There are no shirts and overalls in the stores for midsize boys. Clerks advise us to buy the smallest in men's sizes and cut them down. I wonder how many of them have ever tried to make a big shirt smaller? It would be easier to make two or three new ones than to do that. We are rather busy right now with all those extra duties plus as many letters as possible to be sent to loved ones far away.

To be sure, Bruce is getting along very well right now with a shirt that Charles wore last winter and one of his dad's that shrunk. His well-patched overalls may or may not hold out another week. Irvin lost one of his mittens in the haymow when he was helping load alfalfa to grind for alfalfa meal. He has no shirts at all but wears coveralls. It really would help if somebody would do something about getting shirts and/or overalls plus mittens and/or underwear in boys' sizes on the market again.

YOUR Soap Creeker is here alone today, and it seems very lonely. A while ago a strange thump in the neighborhood of the front porch was quite alarming, although it would have gone unnoticed if the family or the grandchildren had been here. You should have seen this farm woman tiptoe up the stairs and stealthily latch the front door screen—a bit ashamed of being so timid all of a sudden and a bit amused at herself for thinking that latching that dilapidated door would keep out any marauder who might try to steal all those newly canned pickles and beans or the remains of the last ham she was able to find last week while digging around in the vastnesses of that apparently empty pork barrel.

Just for good measure it probably would be a good idea to close the front door to keep out the road dust. The only reason it hasn't been closed today is that the closed door might make any light-fingered passerby think nobody was home and this might be a good time to stop and snoop a while.

In the paragraphs above many of you country women will recognize definite symptoms of a farm wife's first day at home alone for a few days or weeks. No doubt on the first day of school countless screens are latched for the first time in weeks, as all sounds appear unduly loud without the usual accompaniment of young voices at play or work or brotherly or sisterly argument. During haying, which is just over, even though some of the fields were not close to the house loads of hay were brought to the barn at frequent intervals and the head farmer and three tall sons hurried to the house for fresh drinks each time. But today two of the sons are up in the corn country yanking off undesired tassels while their father and eldest brother are at Vaughn's farm threshing all by themselves.

Now the bread is out of the oven and the last jar of pickles is canned, so it is time to go to the garden and pick today's crop of cucumbers. By that time your Soap Creeker may be too tired to think about any intruder who may have wandered into the house while she was gone. Lock the door? No need for that. In a day or two it will seem as natural to be here alone as for the tractor to be putt-putting in the meadow.

Now it is another day. Yesterday's adventures have become a part of the more or less remembered past. No sooner were the beets canned and the last speck of sugar in the sugar jar used than your Soap Creeker decided it was too hot and she was too tired to pick the cucumbers right at that moment. (We think she knew right then she was going to find some excuse to wait until the cool of the morning for this task.) She took the new magazine and went upstairs. Soon callers arrived. As usual they guessed wrong and came to the back door. When nobody is upstairs everybody comes to the front door and are quite distressed because we have to climb the stairs to answer their knock. The next time they come to the back door, and nobody is downstairs. Many who come often shout from the front porch and learn whether we are upstairs or downstairs, although it is easier for us to climb the stairs to let them in than it is for them to go down the steps to the backyard and the back door.

It wouldn't do to let you know I was the first one who tried to get in at the latched front door. Even though I knew—or thought I knew—right where the latch should be, it took me some time to find it when I reached through the torn screen. Maybe a burglar couldn't find it after all.

FORTY-TWO small spotted pigs run and romp with glee over our domain. It matters not to them whether their playground is a flower bed, a cornfield, or the precise spot where a mother hen wishes to scratch out some bugs and worms for her children. Under every gate and between the meshes of the woven wire fences they creep to explore everything that needs to be explored. This is a world of wonders, and while they notice not the sunsets, the beauty of the tree-clad hills, or the havoc the chinch bugs have wrought in the oat fields, they find much that is of interest to them that they have not seen in their few short weeks of life. No fence can hold them; no harsh words can discourage them. The only way to keep them where they are is to feed them so abundantly that they will grow rapidly and become too large to slip through barriers that are supposed to be swine-proof.

Living near the railroad track as we do I've often wondered why drivers take the hills at a breakneck speed when they know by hurrying they will be obliged to wait at the crossing for a long freight train to make its slow way toward Chicago or Kansas City. Doubtless when the car does get across the track, the driver steps heavily upon the footfeed so he can get to the next crossing in time to wait for the same train there.

Few of us are equipped with enough intelligence to hurt us, but methinks Judge Robert Cooper could be rated fairly high on that score. He's the judge in Puerto Rico who ruled that an eight-year-old boy could be a witness even though the lad confessed he didn't understand the meaning of taking an oath. Why? Because when he asked young Juan Rivera what would happen to him if he were to tell a lie, the boy leaned toward the judge and whispered:

"I'd get warts."

L A S T night, for the first time in 1950, blankets, comforters, and quilts were taken off the wardrobe shelves to make a bed for one granddaughter on the living room sofa and for the other in two overstuffed chairs pulled up beside the sofa. The one young lady announced that she was going to sleep with Grandick. Whereupon the other remarked that she didn't want to sleep on that davenport and marched off to bed in a room that already had one occupant. So this morning there were five beds to be made, although two of them had had nobody sleep in them. Do you suppose those people are right who claim that grandparents spoil youngsters? I wouldn't know. I had only one living grandparent in my lifetime, and I don't think we children ever did anything we shouldn't do when he was around. I am sure of that, for he never scolded us for anything we did.

I had gone to the basement to put some cobs on the furnace and fireplace fires when a fuse burned out and all went dark. In my usual rush, before I could get stopped I had dashed into the ironing board; fallen down over the sock box; struck my arm on something sharp as I landed; and spilled my scoop shovel of cobs all over the floor, the small granddaughter, and her mother as Cathy was eating her supper in front of the fireplace. Catherine didn't mind being struck with a few cobs, but she did mind having her mother stop feeding her. While the two sons were getting another fuse in place Granny picked herself up and was by the fireplace when the lights came on. Cathy had to have food at once, but Granny didn't have much more luck with the spoon than with the scoop shovel. The lights went out again, Granny couldn't find Catherine's mouth, and Catherine couldn't find the spoon. Mommy protested that we spilled the soup all over her good dress. So the old grandmother hunted the broom during the next lighted interval. Catherine decided to explore the egg case. Another fuse went the way of the first two, and the startled Catherine shoved the egg back in the general direction of the egg case but it missed and went on the floor.

"Why doesn't someone turn on the lights?" complained three-year-old Diann.

At last the men have finished the rewiring, and once more we can install a regular fuse instead of the weak one that burns out easily to avoid damage if the wrong wires are crossed.

And the two biggest bruises on my arm are on either side of my watch. Doubtless the arm will get well sooner than would the watch if it had received the blow.

RECENTLY I telephoned the daughter-in-law. Three-year-old Catherine answered. Since she doesn't talk at all plainly, stands some distance from the telephone, shouts at the top of her voice, and talks as rapidly as her grandmother (I almost said as rapidly as both her grandmothers at once but that would be impossible, so I'll change that to either of her grandmothers) it isn't a question of understanding *all* of what she says. The problem is understanding *any* of it. I did understand that Mommie wasn't in the house. Then came a long story with pauses only for the teller to catch her breath. At last I understood a whole sentence: "And I got a dolly and Diann got a dolly and Dougie got a tractor."

So I knew she had been talking about the Christmas season. I should have known for she had told me the same story every time I had seen her since Christmas. There was no need to feel hurt because she hadn't mentioned the toy store I had given her and her sister. Maybe she had told me all about it; she had used enough words to have done so twice. Soon there was a pause, so I told her that would be all for this time.

"Call me up again sometime," she invited. No doubt I shall, but I hope I am not too tired the next time. It is very hard work "talking" over the telephone to that young lady.

Once Catherine was spending the night with us. Dick was tired and had gone to bed early. I was quilting, with the young lady sitting beside me talking, talking, talking. After a while there came a groan from the bedroom.

"Will you stuff one of my socks in that girl's mouth so I can go to sleep?" shouted the exasperated farmer.

All was silent for a long moment, with the small girl squirming in embarrassment.

"Dick is your jamfadder, and he is Vaughn's jamfadder, but he isn't my jamfadder," announced Dick's granddaughter as she marched off soberly to bed.